BUILD WITH LIVING STONES

COMPREHENSIVE COURSE ON THE FRANCISCAN MISSION CHARISM

Published in the United States
by Franciscan Institute Publications
St. Bonaventure University, St. Bonaventure, NY 14778

© 2015 Franciscan Institute Publications,
St. Bonaventure University

All rights reserved.
No part of this book may be reproduced or transmitted in any form or by any means, electronic or mechanical, without permission in writing from the publsher.

Cover design by Jill M. Smith

ISBN: 978-1-57659-3691
eISBN: 978-1-57659-370-7

Library of Congress Cataloging-in Publication Data

Build with living stones : formation for Franciscan life and work / edited by Daria Mitchell, OSF. -- Second Edition.
    pages cm
  ISBN 978-1-57659-369-1 (print) -- ISBN 978-1-57659-370-7 (ebook) -- ISBN 978-1-57659-523-7 (epdf) 1. Franciscans--North America. 2. Franciscans--Handbooks, manuals, etc. 3. Franciscans--Study and teaching. I. Mitchell, Daria, editor of compilation.
  BX3607.B85 2013
  255'.3--dc23
                                                              2013045688

Printed and bound in the United States of America
Franciscan Institute Publications makes every effort
to use environmentally responsible suppliers and materials
in the publishing of its books. This book is printed on acid-free, recycled paper
that is FSC (Forest Stewardship Council) certified.
It is printed with soy-based ink.

BUILD WITH LIVING STONES

COMPREHENSIVE COURSE ON THE FRANCISCAN MISSION CHARISM

EDITED BY
SR. DARIA MITCHELL

FRANCISCAN INSTITUTE PUBLICATIONS
ST. BONAVENTURE UNIVERSITY

Build with Living Stones: *Formation of Franciscan Life and Work* is based upon the internationally recognized *Comprehensive Source on the Franciscan Charism*. This updated edition is a valuable resource that gives users a Franciscan view of life and work.

The *new* Build With Living Stones is unique, in that it is genuinely inter-Franciscan. It provides the Franciscan family a creative blend of the best in current theology, Franciscan research and pastoral practice. This new edition also brings together Franciscan experts on Mission and provides resources on Franciscan life and work that are applicable in a North American context.

In September of 1996, The Franciscan Institute at St. Bonaventure University became the new center for *Build With Living Stones*. As such, it provides coordination of various regional programs throughout the United States and Canada, as well as preparatory workshops for teachers and facilitators. In September of 2000, the *Build With Living Stones*: *Formation for Franciscan Life and Work* was initiated. In 2010 a Facilitator's Guide was made available online through the Franciscan Institute Publications website. The New Edition was printed in 2015.

Editorial Board:
        Fr. Michael Cusato
        Sr. Paula Scraba
        Anthony LoGalbo
        Anita Holzmer, OSF
        Ron Pihokker, SFO
        Sr. Kathy Warren, OSF

Production and Design: Jill M. Smith

Introduction

In his book on discipleship, Bishop NT Wright states, "The longer you look at Jesus, the more you will want to serve him in his world."[1] No one demonstrates the truth of that statement more forthrightly than Francis of Assisi. He was a man who began looking at the Lord Jesus, while taken a prisoner of war in his early twenties, and the world he saw was powerfully and refreshingly different from the one in which he grew up.

Looking anew at the Lord Jesus, he saw a world where violence and greed need not be the norm of social and ecclesial relationships. He saw a world that was not divided between the privileged few and the deprived many. He saw a universe no longer bending to the majesty of a cold and distant imperial divinity, but instead one that was ever refreshed and enlivened in the abundance of a good, gracious and abundant God who bent low in mercy towards us.

Francis couldn't get enough of this look upon a humble and close God. The incarnation fascinated Francis. It was so different from the frightening apocalyptic majesty with which he grew up. This more accessible and forgiving God offered him a way to restart and renew his relationships with the world and every creature in it. It provided him with a radical insight into the purpose of his life, the meaning of the world and of his growing band of brothers and sisters. The longer Francis looked at Jesus, the more he invited his followers into a vibrant interdependence with all creation, creating thereby a new ethical space in which to resolve and reconcile differences.

This edition of Build with Living Stones provides a new generation of readers with an opportunity to follow the moments of Francis' conversion, from his disillusionment after the Battle of Collestrada to his embrace of the leper. It will offer an understanding to the meaning of Francis' naked protest before his father and his bishop in the town square. This book will invite readers into Francis' evolving imagination, a narrative that revolutionized Christian and world spirituality in the process.

---

1 NT Wright, *Following Jesus: Biblical Reflections on Discipleship* (Grand Rapids, MI: Wm. B. Eerdmans, 1994), ix.

Francis wanted his followers to greet everyone they met with the words, "peace and all good." It was not a clever slogan or a cheap catchphrase. In his day, people met one another within the social categories of the majores and minores, the have's and the havenot's. By his new greeting, Francis meant to introduce people to the world he had seen by looking at Christ, the world of brother sun and sister moon, the world that was beautiful and diverse, joyous and grand, elegant in the wonder of a God who is good, all good, supremely good, all the time and to everyone. May God give you this wonder! May God give you this peace!

David B. Couturier, OFM. Cap.
Executive Director of Franciscan Institute Publications
Dean, The School of Franciscan Studies
St. Bonaventure University

Lesson Units

1. Francis, Clare, and the Franciscan Family

2. Witnesses to the Incarnation

3. Traces of Trinity

4. The Gospel Way: Moving toward the Reign of God

5. The Franciscan Mission

6. To be Formed into Christ Jesus

7. The Franciscan Evangelist: Developing a Contemplative Consciousness

8. Franciscan Presence and Dialogue: Living with Diversity in a Pluralistic Society

9. Franciscan Peace-Making

10. Inculturation Through a Franciscan Perspective

11. A Franciscan Perspective on the Economy and the Global Reality

12: Gender: Realities, Stumbling Blocks and Breakthroughs

13. Brother Sun and Sister Moon: A Franciscan View of Creation

14. The Franciscan Role in the Church

UNIT ONE

FRANCIS, CLARE
AND THE FRANCISCAN FAMILY

Contents

From the Franciscan Sources

A. Introduction

B. Survey

C. Information

D. Questions

E. Bibliography

From the Franciscan Sources

Brother Masseo, one of Francis's first brothers, was unable to understand why so many people were running after Francis. His followers came from every walk of life: young and old, men and women, educated and unlettered, married and single, from among the nobility and the peasantry alike. All wanted to walk the way of Francis. "What could it be?" Masseo wondered, "what is it that attracts all these people?"

Francis was not an educated man; he knew how to read and write, but not much else. He did not have an instantly recognizable family name, nor could he boast of a noble heritage. He was merely the son of a merchant. Nor was Francis good looking; he was small and almost repulsive to look at, with ears that stuck out. Clearly, it was neither his education, background nor personal beauty that attracted so many people. So what was it? Brother Masseo repeated his thoughts to Francis himself. When Francis heard them, he rejoiced, "If none of those things matter," he cried, "then it is God himself who attracts them; it is because of him that all these people follow me." (Based on *The Little Flowers of St. Francis*[1]).

A. Introduction

Francis and Clare had an incarnational faith firmly grounded in the enfleshment of the Word into the world. Sharing a common calling, God "gave" them countless brothers and sisters (cf. Test 14).

Today, too, there are those who have committed themselves to one of the four Rules of Franciscan Life and still others who share the vision of these two Saints without a public profession.

---
[1] *FA:ED* 3, 583.

The words Clare left for her sisters are relevant to all of these:

> Among the gifts we received and daily continue to receive from the Father of mercies, our Benefactor, is our calling, for which we must express our deepest thanks to our glorious God. Therefore, the Apostle wrote: "Know your calling!" The Son of Man has been designated the Way which our blessed Father Francis, his true lover and imitator, has shown and taught us by word and example (TestCl 1ff).

Our common calling is based upon the Baptism which we share along with our desire to witness together in today's societies in the spirit of Francis and Clare. This vision is more urgent than ever, as we will see.

B. Survey

The lives and example of Francis and Clare have had a marvelous and far-reaching effect, providing a unique and energizing way to live the Gospel we were committed to in our baptism.

Francis worked out such a way of life for himself without any intention of attracting followers. However, brothers were then "given [to] him" (cf.Test 14). Later, through Clare's commitment, women joined the movement. In addition, there were others who, while not desiring a vowed commitment, wanted to live in the spirit of Francis and Clare. Soon enough, these developed into three Orders with four Rules along with many lay people participating in spirit in the Franciscan movement. Thus the Franciscan family developed, women and men of every walk of life following the Gospel after the pattern of these two pivotal Saints.

This, then, is the origin of those who are inspired to travel the Franciscan way, uniting into one common family, in order to witness more effectively to their Gospel calling. The history of the development of this family is extremely complex, filled with disputes and developments as in any family.

It reminds one of the colorful account that Gary Nebhan paints in his book, *Songbirds, Truffles, and Wolves*:

> In the piazza centrale, stood seven old-timers with their canes, potbellies, gestures, and stories. I went up to the closest one and asked him directions to the official Strada Francescana.
>
> "We're pilgrims. Which is the way pilgrims have taken when walking to Assisi?
>
> Before my contact could answer, arms shot out pointing in every direction. Seven different answers came at once out of seven different mouths, and as they heard each other's recommended directions, their faces filled with color and expression.
>
> "What do you mean, turn left at the next street? The bridge on that street has been closed down for months now!"
>
> Disgusted, another man waved them all off, grabbed Ginger and me by the shoulders, and marched us out into the middle of the main street, where he hobbled along with us until we arrived at the lane where he wanted us to turn. He patted me on the back and grumbled, "There it is, my friends, now go, before the others try to change your minds."
>
> I looked back at his six cronies, and they were still arguing. Waving their arms, shaking their canes, and making dramatic gestures to one another with their hands. I had to laugh; we had asked them too large and weighty a question for an afternoon in the week before

the Festa di San Francesco: "What is the true Franciscan way?"[2]

One can be forgiven if he or she thinks they are present at a convention of Franciscan historians as they read this amusing account. Today, however, we recognize that the "true Franciscan way" necessarily admits of diversity and pluralism.

C. INFORMATION

The Franciscan Movement did not develop in a vacuum. Its seeds are historically obvious in other evangelical movements of the times.

When Francis spoke of his new life, he used the word penance. Logically enough, then, the original name for his band of followers was the "penitents of Assisi". Clare also saw herself as a penitent. Penance is a vital concept for an understanding of their period of history. For them, it was synonymous with living according to the Gospel, denoting a total commitment to God and Jesus Christ.

The medieval concept of penance shaped religious awareness in the twelfth and thirteenth centuries. It emphasized separation from the rest of society in order to live in a special relationship with God, individually or communally. Penitents' understanding of their calling was that they should grieve constantly for their own sins and the sins of everyone else. Through a life of prayer, meditation and self-denial, they were seeking their own salvation and that of others.

Sin and forgiveness were seen by these Christians to affect more than the isolated individual. Rather, it affected the entire Body of Christ. The Church, therefore, regarded penance as a public act. The public role of defining sin and granting forgiveness as well as imposing penalties was taken up by the Church. For murder, adultery, and apostasy, acts of penance must be performed. These acts include abstention from sex within marriage, donations to the poor, endowments to churches and monasteries, recitation of certain prayers, and fasting. Gradually

---

[2] Nebhan, Gary Paul, *Songbirds, Truffles and Wolves: An American Naturalist in Italy* (New York: Penguin Books, 1993), 169-70.

public penance was replaced by private confession, even though the institutional Church opposed such a move. Many women and men opted to continue a public penitential way of life that they freely embraced, making reparation not only for their own sins but also for the sins of others. Eventually many public penitents were hired by others to do their penances for them. Among these penances were fasting on Mondays, Wednesdays, and Fridays; keeping the Great Fast during Lent; almsgiving; self-inflicted pain, for example hairshirts and flagellations; retreats; and pilgrimages.

Francis's view of Gospel living was certainly influenced by the penitential movement and, in turn, it influenced the penitents deeply. The Secular Franciscan Order had its origins among the penitents. The movement had most of its effect among women. Throughout central Italy, there was a spontaneous growth of such organizations for and among women. These mostly involved women of noble or landed family background, called to a radical life for God, to be lived in solitude or often in a convent.

It is understandable, then, that ascetic motivations characterized the Franciscan movement. Yet it is not asceticism that lies at the center of this movement. The emphasis of the Franciscan way is above all a positive one: witness to a God who became human and who makes human beings more fully themselves.

The sociopolitical situation in Assisi played a decisive role in the way Francis and Clare developed this positive emphasis.

In his Testament, Francis divides his life into two distinct phases: his "life in sin" and his "life of penance." It was the common parlance of his times to indicate what Francis called "the exodus from the world." Francis understood his own later life as a definite reversal of the life which he had previously led among the townspeople of Assisi.

To understand the fascination Francis exerted on so many people, we need to examine his "life in sin." In describing the early life of Francis, we are tempted to understand the state of sin in terms of his personal sins. But this phrase is primarily meant to express a general state of sinfulness, a complete reliance on society's values along with relationships that were untouched by the Gospel. Much urban life at the time, though, was shaped by the presence of churches and priests and by participation in divine services. These two mindsets pulled against one another, at times creating a certain schizophrenia that eventually led to a philosophical dualism.

This world into which Francis was born can be characterized by the following indicators:

- The majority of the population lived at the subsistence level with countless people suffering poverty and misery. The worst lot fell to the lepers who were forced to live outside of town boundaries. The Church even had services that formally excluded them from daily life in the towns.

- Urban development was leading to mass abandonment of life on the land. The basis of society was no longer the land but towns. With the rise of towns, there arose an urban self-confidence that rejected feudal rule, power deriving from ownership of land, and reliance on a mutual loyalty between master and servant.

- In 1203, the Peace Charter was signed between the nobility and the people of Assisi. It reaffirmed government by the nobility but in the mildest form.

- In 1210, a Freedom Charter was presented to Assisi, shifting the weight of power back to the common people.

One can immediately see the impact that growing up in Assisi had upon Francis, for, when he "left the world," it was this world. He accepted poverty freely and embraced the outcast leper; he preached peace without reference to classes; and he sought approval of his own freedom charter before the Pope.

But it was the leper who became the immediate source of Francis's conversion. He recognized that Assisi was essentially a "culture without compassion:" the social system in which he had grown up was not based upon Gospel values, even though it was culturally Catholic. This world was rooted in money, prestige, and power as well as the rule of the rich over the poor. So Francis distanced himself from this world to develop his alternative "culture of compassion," rooted in the Gospel (cf. Test 1-5), discovering the Crucified in the lepers and the poor. It is this culture that the contemporary Franciscan Movement seeks to continue and strengthen.

At first Francis remained alone. But a culture cannot be developed alone. Others joined him in this alternative way of living. Witness Thomas of Celano (1C 36ff), writing in 1229:

> Men ran, woman also ran, clerics hurried, and religious rushed to see and hear the holy one of God, who seemed to everyone a person of another age. People of all ages and both sexes hurried to behold the wonders which the Lord worked anew in the world through his servant.... Many people, well-born and lowly, cleric and lay, driven by divine inspiration began to come to Saint Francis.... To all he gave a norm of life and to those of every rank he sincerely pointed out the way to salvation.

Writing in a letter in 1216, Jacques de Vitry provides an eyewitness account from outside the Franciscan Movement itself:

> ... After I had been at the Curia for a while, I encountered a great deal that was repugnant to me. They were so occupied with worldly affairs, with rulers and kingdoms, with lawsuits and litigation, that they hardly let anyone speak of spiritual things. I did find, however, one source of consolation in those parts. Many well-to-do secular people of both sexes, having left all things for Christ, had fled the world. They were called "Lesser Brothers" and "Lesser Sisters." They are held in great reverence by the Lord Pope and the Cardinals. They are in no way occupied with temporal things, but with fervent desire and ardent zeal they labor each day to draw from the vanities of

the world souls that are perishing, and draw them to their way of life. Thanks be to God, they have already reaped great fruit and have converted many. Those who have heard them, say: "Come," so that one group brings another.

They live according to the form of the primitive Church, about whom it was written: *The community of believers were of one heart and one mind.* During the day they go into the cities and villages giving themselves over to the active life in order to gain others; at night, however, they return to their hermitage or solitary places to devote themselves to contemplation. The women dwell together near the cities in various hospices, accepting nothing, but living by the work of their hands. They are grieved, indeed troubled, by the fact that they are honored by both clergy and laity more than they would wish.[3]

Clare of Assisi is the second founding figure of this new spiritual outlook. The nineteenth century scholar Sabatier rightly observed that "The figure of Clare is not merely a reproduction of Francis.... She had a clear sense of the shape of her own spirituality before she ever came in contact with Francis."

Francis's family belonged to the newly emerging merchant class, which was a third class developing between the maiores (the nobility) and the minores, (the poor and common folk). On the otherhand, Clare's family was a member of the maiores. Once Clare was established at San Damiano, her blood sisters Agnes and Beatrice, her mother Ortolana and another relative Pacifica di Guelfuccio, all followed her there. For these Sisters Minor, as they were initially known, Francis wrote a *forma vitae* (form of life), which Clare eventually adopted into the text of her own Rule.

---

[3] *Francis of Assisi: Early Franciscan Documents* (Hyde Park: New City Press, 1999),Vol. 1, 579-80. Jacques de Vitry, Letter written in Genoa in 1216 to his friends in Liege, cited in *CA:ED*, 428.

When the Blessed Francis saw that we had no fear of poverty, hard work, suffering, shame, or contempt of the world, but that, instead, we regarded such things as great delights, moved by compassion he wrote for us the following form of life: 'Since by divine inspiration you have made yourselves daughters and servants of the most high King, Father, and have taken the Holy Spirit as your spouse, choosing to live according to the perfection of the Holy Gospel, I resolve and promise for myself and for my brothers always to have that same loving care and special solicitude for you as I have for them' (RCl 6:2).

This way of life was unknown to the Church of Clare's time. The only recognized model for religious women was a Benedictine monastic lifestyle which predated the Franciscan Movement and to which the Church bound all religious women. Clare struggled to establish her claim to the Franciscan way of life that emphasized absolute poverty, thus rejecting the Church's law that women's communities had to have material possessions and endowments. After a long and stubborn fight with the Roman Curia, Clare prevailed and wrote her own Rule, approved by the Pope shortly before her death. Thus she became the first woman in history to have written a Rule for an order of women.

Francis and Clare were an integral part of a wider penitential movement that helped to form their ideas and spirituality. Their personalities attracted people from all walks of life and social strata who wanted to share their evangelical vision and live it in their daily lives. Out of their appeal to others emerged followers, some of whom joined one of the four established Orders and others who, while not following any one of the Rules, followed their inspiration. The picture, then, is that of a many-faceted community made up of people who wanted to share in the alternative way offered by Francis and Clare, and who found their identity, meaning, and individuality through their encounter with these Saints.

Francis welcomed all those who wanted to pattern their lives after him, uniting them in a common bond of Gospel living. While Francis wanted to reach out to them personally, he was not able to do so. Instead he wrote two letters to all the faithful. These letters are still available to us and challenge us to pursue the Gospel to which we were committed at our Baptism.

D. QUESTIONS

1. What do the stories of Francis and Clare have to do with us? How committed am I to be in dialogue with Francis, Clare, and the stories of this tradition in order to frame my way of living in the world?

2. Who are the storytellers that I listen to for inspiration and enlightenment?

3. Think of some Franciscan men and women by whom I have been inspired. What is it that inspires me?

4. How would you describe Gospel life? What do you feel are the basic values that are part of Gospel living?

5. What is new information from this Unit that affirms my priorities? What information challenges my priorities?

6. What questions does this Unit raise for me?

E. BIBLIOGRAPHY

Basic Reference for the entire BWLS Program includes the following four texts:

Francis of Assisi: Early Documents, Volumes 1-3. Ed. Regis J. Armstrong, J.A. Wayne Hellmann and William J. Short. New York: New City Press.

Volume 1: The Saint, 1999.
Volume 2: The Founder, 2000.

Volume 3: The Prophet, 2001.
(Henceforth referred to as FA:ED.)

Clare of Assisi: Early Documents. The Lady. Ed., trans. Regis J. Armstrong. New York: New City Press, 2006. (Henceforth referred to as CA:ED.)

Additional Bibliography for this unit:

House, Adrian. *Francis of Assisi: A Revolutionary Life*. Mahwah, NJ: Hidden Spring, 2000.
Reluctant Saint: The Life of Francis of Assisi. New York: Viking Compass, 2002.

F. PICTURE CREDIT
  Francis and Clare of Assisi, upper basilica, San Francesco, Assisi

UNIT TWO

WITNESSES TO THE INCARNATION

Build With Living Stones 15

CONTENTS

From the Franciscan Sources

A. Introduction

B. Survey

C. Information

D. Questions

E. Bibliography

F. Picture Credits

From the Franciscan Sources

It happened, three years prior to his death, that Francis decided to celebrate at the town of Greccio the memory of the birth of the Child Jesus with the greatest possible solemnity, in order to arouse devotion. So that this would not be considered a type of novelty, he petitioned for and obtained permission from the Supreme Pontiff.

> He had a manger prepared, hay carried in and an ox and an ass led to the spot. The brethren are summoned, the people arrive, the forest amplifies with their cries, and that venerable night is rendered brilliant and solemn by the multitude of bright lights and by the resonant and harmonious hymns of praise.
>
> The man of God stands before the manger, filled with piety, bathed in tears, and overcome with joy. A solemn Mass is celebrated over the manger, with Francis, a levite of Christ, chanting the holy Gospel. Then he preaches to the people standing around him about the birth of the poor King, whom, whenever he means to call him, he called in his tender love, the Babe from Bethlehem (LMj 10:7).

A. Introduction

Francis and Clare of Assisi lived their faith in Christ in a way that would make human beings more human and this world a better place in which to live. With them, we witness to a God who is involved in this world. We point to a mystery that is present, so we note that in St. Bonaventure's retelling of the Greccio account, it is not a past experience but an ongoing one, made clear by Bonaventure through his use of the present tense: "The brethren are summoned … the people arrive ... the forest amplifies ... that venerable night is rendered ... the man of God stands ... a solemn Mass is celebrated ... then he preaches."[1]

It is from this experience of the Incarnation that Franciscans from around the globe grapple with the questions: what is our task? What significance do we have in the world? And what significance does the world have for us?

After all is said and done, we are an incarnational people, who take seriously the words of Jesus: "You are the light of the world," "You are the salt of the earth," and "You are a city built on a hill." We have a message. We have a vision of life that we want to share and a way of life for which many are searching.

B. Survey

During this session we will be introduced to the reflections of some writers outside the Franciscan family who have much to say about the Franciscan perspective on life and work. They often look at our origins with an immediacy that we might have lost. From this renewed insight, we will rediscover the secular character of the Franciscan calling. But we must first clarify the meaning of secular in the light of Francis's regard for the whole world as his cloister, that is, as a place where he could discover his Incarnate Lord. Sometimes we lose sight of this original insight that is obvious in the incarnational outlook of Francis and Clare.

Understanding the repercussions of this incarnational spirituality will help us begin to appreciate the Franciscan meaning of mission and evangelization.

C. Information

Understood properly, the Franciscan way of life is secular. This does not mean that it is godless or secularized. Quite the opposite. God created the world in such a way that we might find the divine in creation. Jesus took human form so that we might discover the intermingling of the divine with

---

[1] *Francis of Assisi: Early Documents*, Vol. 2 (New York: New City Press, 2000), 610.

the human. The divine, then, is found in all things except sin: in ordinary people with their desires and needs; in our concrete situations and social circumstances; in the events of our lives and our daily experiences; on city streets and country gardens. The Christian need not leave the world to meet God. He or she need only to use his or her sanctified senses, as St. Bonaventure reminds us about Francis: "... the entire fabric of the universe came to the service of the sanctified senses of the holy man" (LMj 5:12). And in his masterpiece *The Soul's Journey into God*, he observes:

> Whoever is not enlightened by [the] splendor of created things is blind; whoever is not awakened by such outcries is deaf; whoever does not praise God because of all these effects is dumb; whoever does not discover the First Principle from such clear signs is a fool. Therefore, open your eyes, alert the ears of your spirit, open your lips and apply your heart so that in all creatures you may see, hear, praise, love and worship, glorify and honor your God (1:15).[2]

Unfortunately, during the history of the Christian churches, a dualism developed that distinguished between the world and the spirit. World and spirit were often presented as predominately in conflict one with the other. So a spirituality emerged that encouraged one to despise the body, mortify the senses, flee the world in order to abandon oneself to God, focus on the spirit, and awaken the world within. An irreconcilable contrast was created.

This dualism cannot serve as the orientation of Franciscan life, even though we must admit that, in some ways, it existed in Francis and Clare. It can be clearly seen in Francis's attitude toward his body, which he disciplined severely and called "Brother Ass." Yet, we are reminded by St. Bonaventure that "[Francis] had reached such purity that his flesh was in remarkable harmony with his spirit and his spirit with God" (LMj5:9). Further the author of the Mirror of Perfection puts

---

[2] St. Bonaventure, *The Soul's Journey into God*, trans, and intro. by Ewert Cousins, Classics of Western Spirituality (New York: Paulist Press, 1978),1:15.

these words in Francis's mouth: "Wherever we are, or wherever we go, we always take our cell with us; for Brother Body is our cell, and our soul is the hermit who lives in it" (2MP 65). Of course there were dichotomies in Francis's thinking; he was a man of his time.

Yet it is equally obvious that Francis experienced God in the world: in the embrace of the outcast, a poor despised person and in the encounter with the social misery that he discovers in individuals and institutions. Francis rejected the heartless world based on exclusiveness and entered a compassionate world founded on inclusiveness. In order to bring about the transformation of society that Francis dreamed possible he commanded his brothers to "go through the world ... [living] according to the spirit of the Gospel" (cf. ER 14). So Francis did not literally leave the world but regarded it as the place of his new life.

In the great mystery play Francis and Lady Poverty, written by an unknown author in the thirteenth century, Lady Poverty asks Francis and his brothers where their cloister is. They reply with a sweeping gesture of their hands, showing her the whole world as far as she could see and say: "This, Lady, is our cloister" (ScEx 63). Francis's great poem *The Canticle of Brother Sun* is a hymn that expresses a fully realized secular spirituality.

It would be helpful to read the writings of St. Francis in a worldly way since these rules and letters provide us with a way "to go about the world," providing us with a way of being in the world as evangelists rather than running from the world as recluses.

To understand the worldliness of a Franciscan approach to life we need to investigate why St. Francis called Christmas "the feast of all feasts" (2C 199). This statement would antagonize many a contemporary liturgist, who would be quick to remind us that Easter is the greatest feast of the Church year. However, for Francis, as is obvious from the Greccio experience, the Incarnation is the greatest of all mysteries, for it is a mystery on which he based his life. There is little doubt that the average Christian would agree with Francis rather than the liturgists.

No theologian spoke more lovingly and eloquently about the Incarnation than John Duns Scotus, the faithful fourteenth century follower of St. Francis. Scotus takes as his point of departure the love of God. For him, God is indeed love. God, perfect self-giving, is revealed both in the doctrine of the Trinity and the Incarnation.

For Scotus, creation is not an afterthought in God's mind nor is the Incarnation a result of sin. Rather God created the world, and particularly human persons, patterned after Christ Jesus, "the firstborn of all creation" (Col 1:15). In this, Scotus is not only a follower of Francis but also a follower of St. Paul, particularly in his letters to the Colossians and the Ephesians. God wants the world of creatures to be founded on love, on perfect self-giving. Creation is a network of relationships, a reality that is defined through relatedness and solidarity. Just as "God so loved the world that he sent his only begotten Son," (John 3:16) so we are called to love the world and be sent into it.

This is why St. Francis discovered and celebrated the presence of God in the world. For him, the Incarnation reveals God as Deus Minor, the humble one whom Francis met in littleness: in a child who was born in a stable, in the midst of the homeless and the vulnerable, in the aged and the infirm, in the plight of anyone harmed by a harsh economy that values the rich over the poor.

Just as Jesus was sent, Christmas presented Francis with the challenge of being sent into the world. He reminded his brothers of this mission:

> As you announce peace with your mouth, make sure that greater peace is in your hearts. Let no one be provoked to anger or scandal through you, but may everyone be drawn to peace, kindness, and harmony through your gentleness. For we have been called to this: to heal the wounded, bind up the broken, and recall the erring. In

fact, many who seem to us to be members of the devil will yet be disciples of Christ (3C 14:58).

The Incarnation, then, is the basis for the humanization of the person and of society. The experience of this mystery implies a daily conversion from the usual order of values to a radical change in human behavior. What was considered small and insignificant is now recognized as large and significant; and what appeared as great and valuable will now be ranked as unimportant and valueless. This conversion is learning to think as God thinks and to see as God sees, for God's thoughts are different from those of human beings. The lepers belong in the center, the powerful on the margins.

Perhaps G. K. Chesterton expresses this Franciscan phenomenon best when he writes of Francis:

> The man who went into the cave was not the man who came out again; in that sense he was almost as different as if he were dead, as if he were a ghost or a blessed spirit. And the effects of this on his attitude towards the actual world were really as extravagant as any parallel can make them. He looked at the world as differently from other men as if he had come out of that dark hole walking on his hands (St. Francis of Assisi).[3]

In seeing the world upside down, Francis saw it as God sees it! Only those who, like God, involve themselves in this world can see it as God sees it. Those who believe in the implications of the Incarnation and witness to it, experience God as powerfully active in history. God and his world are inseparable.

Clare of Assisi also witnessed to this mystery of the Incarnation. She pursued and deepened the mystical thought of St. Francis. In a letter, Francis defined the faithful as "mothers of God." Like Mary, we are called to conceive, carry in our hearts and bodies and give birth to Jesus through our actions. In this way we share in making the presence of God

---

[3] G.K. Chesterton, *St. Francis of Assisi of Assisi* (New York: Doubleday, 1954), 102-03.

in the world more visible (2LtF 53). Clare adopted this thought, writing to Agnes of Prague:

> Love him totally who gave himself totally for your love. His beauty the sun and moon admire, and of his gifts there is no limit in abundance, preciousness and magnitude. I am speaking of him who is the Son of the Most High, whom the virgin brought to birth and remained a virgin after his birth. Cling to his most sweet Mother who carried a Son whom the heavens could not contain; and yet she carried him in the little enclosure of her holy womb and held him on her virginal lap (3 LAg 15-19).

Incredibly, the Unlimited became limited. God lives in the limitations of creation and incarnation, thus being given into the hands of those whom he created.

Clare carries this thought even further:

> Is it not clear that the soul of the faithful person, the most worthy of all creatures because of the grace of God, is greater than heaven itself? For heaven with the rest of creation cannot contain their Creator. Only the faithful soul is his dwelling place and his throne, and this is possible only through the charity which the wicked do not have. He who is the truth has said: "Whoever loves me will be loved by my Father and I too will love him, and we will come to him and make our dwelling place with him" [John 14:21] ... Therefore, as the glorious Virgin of virgins carried Christ materially in her body, you, too, by following in his footsteps, especially those of poverty and humility, can, without any doubt, always carry him spiritually in your chaste and virginal body; and you will hold him by whom you and all things are held together, thus possessing that which, in comparison with the transitory possessions of this world, you will possess securely (3 LAg 21-26).

Later St. Bonaventure informs us that, having "had the opportunity to withdraw for a short while from the turmoil of distracting thoughts," he desired to reflect upon the Incarnation. The result of this personal retreat is the wonderfully feminine approach to God, *The Five Feasts of the Child Jesus*, in which Bonaventure spiritually conceives, gives birth to, names, adores with the Magi, and presents the Child Jesus in the temple.

Francis, Clare, and Bonaventure teach us from their personal experience that what happened to Mary physically and historically happens for each believing Christian on the mystical and spiritual level. The Incarnation, the indwelling of the Lord in the human person, is a now experience. And, just as the historical moment of the Incarnation was not an experience to be savored by the individual alone but also had profound repercussions for society, so this spiritual moment of Incarnation cannot be limited to the personal level but also has meaning for the world in which we live. No misery, no powerlessness, no need is foreign to the Word made flesh, after whom all that exists is patterned.

This emphasis on the Incarnation gives the Franciscan Movement a unique understanding of its call to be in the world, not as a highly structured army but as a group of Jongleurs de Dieu, to borrow an image from Chesterton.

In 1927, the Jesuit Peter Lippert provided an insight to the Franciscan approach to life, when he wrote:

> The principle that led, through Benedict to Dominic and on to Ignatius, to the organization of more recent congregations seems to be nearing the term of its inner possibilities of development. This does not mean to say, of course, that it will ever be superfluous or replaceable. But a fundamentally new guideline, sought for by so many, and experimented in new foundations, especially today, can probably be found on quite a different track, namely that of the primitive Franciscan ideal: unhampered vivaciousness in a free community of love, that expresses itself spontaneously without being forced into the mould of prescriptions and ordinances, developing personalities according to their own essential nature, both vital and

original, obeying their own inmost law of discipline and self-command. If God should grace His Church one day with an Order of the future, for which so many of the best are yearning today, then it will probably bear the imprint of St. Francis's inspiration (Lippert ll).[4]

Another Jesuit has associated Lippert's reflection with the achievements and insights gained during the Second Vatican Council. Mario von Galli, in his work *Living our Future: Francis of Assisi and the Church of Tomorrow,* maintains that Francis of Assisi has been the secret theme of the Council and that the Church wants to take the path of Francis, in spite of the fact that at times we may feel like Masseo being twirled around at an intersection by today's leaders.[4]

D. QUESTIONS

1. How did Francis and Clare image God? How do I experience God in my life? What activities in my life seem to draw me to God?

2. When am I least aware of God's presence in my life? What activities seem to pull me away from God?

3. Where do I need to be more attentive to the God dimension in my life?

4. How can I look with "new eyes" to witness a God who is involved in this world?

5. How do I see my body as part of my spirituality?

---

[4] Mario von Galli, *Living our Future: Francis of Assisi and the Church of Tomorrow*, trans. Maureen Sullivan and John Drury (Chicago: Franciscan Herald Press, 1976).

E. Bibliography

Boff, Leonardo. *Francis of Assisi: A Model for Human Liberation.* Maryknoll: Orbis, 2006.

Delio, Ilia. *Clare of Assisi: A Heart Full of Love.* Cincinnati: St. Anthony Messenger Press, 2007.

F. Picture Credits

Francis celebrating the Nativity at Greccio, fresco, Giotto, 1223, Upper Church, St. Francis Basilica, Assisi.

Unit Three

Traces of the Trinity

CONTENTS

From the Franciscan Sources

A.   Introduction

B.   Survey

C.   Information

D.   Questions

E.   Bibliography

F.   Picture Credits

From the Franciscan Sources

> Rising at daybreak they [Francis, Bernard of Quintavale, and Peter Catania] went to the church of San Nicolo next to the piazza of the city of Assisi. They entered for prayer, but, because they were simple, they did not know how to find the passage in the gospel about renunciation. They prayed devoutly that the Lord would show them his will on opening the book the first time.
>
> Once they had finished prayer, blessed Francis took the closed book and, kneeling before the altar, opened it. At its first opening, the Lord's counsel confronted them: "If you wish to be perfect, go, sell everything you possess and give to the poor, and you will have a treasure in heaven."
>
> Blessed Francis was overjoyed when he read this passage and thanked God. But since he was a true worshipper of the Trinity, he desired it to be confirmed by a threefold affirmation. He opened the book a second and third time. When he opened it the second time he saw: "Take nothing for your journey," etc., and at the third opening: "If any man wishes to come after me, he must deny himself," etc.
>
> Each time he opened the book, blessed Francis thanked God for confirming his plan and the desire he had conceived earlier. After a third divine confirmation was pointed out and explained, he said to those men, Bernard and Peter: "Brothers, this is our life and rule and that of all who will want to join our company. Go, therefore, and fulfill what you have heard" (L3C 28b-29).

A. Introduction

This account from the *Legend of the Three Companions* may initially strike one as nothing more than a superstitious act. Upon reflection, however, we discover its depth. It is an enlightening account of Francis's belief in the presence of the Trinity[1] in his life and mission, which provides him with insight into his relationships not only with his brothers and sisters but with all creation as well. St. Bonaventure, reflecting on Francis's experience, makes the mystery of the Trinity the cornerstone of his theology of mission: like Jesus we are sent to enter into healing relationships with all with whom we come into contact.[2]

B. Survey

Jesus' mission is anchored in his relationship with the Father, giving us the model for Franciscan fraternity-on-mission: "That they may be one as we are one" (John 17:11). This desire that Jesus expresses is fulfilled when we accept our unity as well as our diversity of Father, Word, and Spirit. Responding to the Father's love, "the Word becomes flesh" (John 1:14) so "that we may have life and have it abundantly" (John 10:10). The abundance of life is the life of the Trinity lived daily through the gifts of the Holy Spirit.

The Franciscan approach to fraternity-on-mission is much greater than the schools, hospitals, and churches that

---

[1] The icon of the Trinity by Andrei Rublev (1370-1430) "... shows the Trinity in the form of three angels. The prototype for this icon was the mysterious appearance of the Holy Trinity in the form of three travelers to Abraham and Sarah under the oak of Mamre. The Church specifically chose this particular icon because it most fully expresses the dogma of the Holy Trinity: the three angels are depicted in equal dignity, symbolizing the tri-unity and equality of all three Persons.

"In Andrei Rublev's icon, the persons of the Holy Trinity are shown in order in which they are confessed in the Credo. The first angel is the first person of the Trinity, God the Father; the second, middle angel is God the Son; the third angel is God the Holy Spirit. All three angels are blessing the chalice, in which lies the sacrificed calf, prepared for eating. The sacrifice of the calf signifies the Savior's death on the cross, while its preparation as food symbolizes the sacrament of the Eucharist. All three angels have staffs in their hand as a symbol of their divine power."

Franciscans have built, staffed and energized through the years. The rebuilding project of Francis, Clare, and their numerous followers was built on much firmer ground. Life together, where brothers and sisters recognize one another as pursuing divine and human relationships in such a way as to echo Jesus' prayer for our oneness, grounds Franciscan life and mission.

Our divine and human relationships reflect the life of the Trinity and provide us with a vision of a life where the Trinity is revealed in our daily existence and encounters. Francis reveals this in his *Canticle of the Creatures* and it is also marvelously reflected in *Urban Canticle*, Sr. Fran McManus's urbanization of the Canticle:

> Now may our God be praised in glass, concrete and steel.
> Scaffolds like Jacob's ladder stretch busily from land to sky;
> Father's power, Spirit's stirrings. Christ lordship revealed.
>
> Visible in human designs that reach, recoil, shift and heal,
> Transfigure urban dreamers as they ride, run, limp or fly;
> Now may our God be praised in glass, concrete and steel.
>
> Fishers of men, women, children vendors lure and reel them in with sales of comfort and joy, aroma of pizza pie.
> Father's power, Spirit stirrings, Christ's lordship revealed,
>
> In the steady beat of stop lights and concrete football, feel the Sacred Heart pulsing. Babies cry, street preachers testify.
> Now may our God be praised in glass, concrete and steel.
>
> Choirs sound: horns honk, teens laugh, rap dreams; bells peal;
> Eagles and falcons brood and breed, their mere, skyscrapers high.
> Father's power, Spirit stirrings, Christ's lordship revealed.

Parks, factories, industry and art stand, sacrament and seal –
God's handiwork working out the promised land, sanctified.
Now may our God be praised in glass, concrete and steal:
Father's power, Spirit's stirrings, Christ's lordship revealed.[3]

As seen in these verses, Sister Fran, like St. Bonaventure, is able to discern the life and energy of the Trinity in ordinary people and events she daily encounters in city life. As a result, she is able to relate to them rather than simply pass them by.

C. Information

When Francis began to travel the Gospel road, he had a sense of "being sent." The Holy Spirit inspired Francis's call to mission; he responded, as did Mary, with his personal "Fiat." The Spirit's invitation to Francis and his followers was a call to be part of a living process, a stream of life, which flows with the living water of baptism, calling us to become one with all of creation as we discover vestiges of Triune life in all creation.

However, Francis was also acutely and personally aware of divisions, some caused by the Gospel itself, as in the case of his relationship with his father. Francis felt that the basis for healing these divisions was not a proselytizing mission but rather a ministry of presence. Quite simply, Francis was called to be present to others as the Trinity is present to us, quietly transforming us through personal relationship.

Francis reached out to others, then, in a number of ways, even through letters exuberantly addressed to "all Christian religious people, clergy and laity, men and women, to all who are in the whole world." Francis writes to all of them "because I am the servent of all, I am obliged to serve all and to administer the fragrant words of my Lord to them" (2LtF 1-2). Thus he passes on what comes from the heart of God, from the inner mystery of

---

[3] Fran McManus,

the Trinity. Just as Jesus was sent into the world by the Father, so too is Francis: to serve, not to be served.

In the *Earlier Rule*, Chapter XXIII, the Poverello shares with us a uniquely beautiful prayer of thanksgiving. Here we perceive the exuberance of Francis's prayer of life. Even more, we discover the manner in which Francis is able to unite his incarnational spirituality with his intense Trinitarian outlook. It is, then, a text worth lingering over:

> All powerful, most holy, Almighty and supreme God, Holy and just Father, Lord King of heaven and earth, we thank You for Yourself for through Your holy will and through Your only Son with the Holy Spirit, you have created everything spiritual and corporal and, after making us in Your own image and likeness, You placed us in paradise. Through our own fault, we fell.
>
> We thank you, for through Your Son, You created us and with holy love You loved us, You brought about His birth as true God and true man by the glorious, ever-virgin, most blessed, holy Mary and You willed to redeem us captives through His cross and blood and death.
>
> We thank You for Your Son Who will come again in the glory of His majesty to send into the eternal fire the wicked ones who have not done penance and have not known You and to say to all those who have known You, adored You and served You in penance: "Come, you blessed of my Father, receive the Kingdom prepared for you from the beginning of the world."
>
> Because all of us, wretches and sinners, are not worthy to pronounce Your name, we humbly ask our Lord Jesus Christ, Your beloved Son in Whom You were well pleased, together with the Holy Spirit, the Paraclete, to give You thanks, for everything as it pleases You and Him, Who always satisfies You in everything, through Whom You have done so much for us.

Because of Your love, we humbly beg the glorious Mother, the most blessed, ever-virgin Mary, Blessed Michael, Gabriel and Raphael, all the choirs of the blessed seraphim, cherubim, thrones, dominations, principalities, powers, virtues, angels, archangels, Blessed John the Baptist, John the Evangelist, Peter, Paul, the blessed patriarchs and prophets, the innocents, apostles, evangelists, disciples, the martyrs, confessors and virgins, the blessed Elijah and Henoch, all the saints who were, who will be, and who are to give You thanks for these things, as it pleases You, God true and supreme, eternal and living, your most beloved Son, our Lord Jesus Christ, and the Holy Spirit, the Paraclete.

All of us lesser brothers, useless servants, humbly ask and beg those who wish to serve the Lord God within the holy Catholic and Apostolic Church and all the following orders: priests, deacons, subdeacons, acolytes, exorcists, lectors, porters, and all clerics, all religious men and women, all penitents and youth, the poor and the needy, kings and princes, workers and farmers, servants and masters, all virgins, continent and married women, all lay people, men and women, all children and adolescents, young and old, the healthy and the sick, all the small and the great, all peoples, races, tribes, and tongues, all nations and all peoples everywhere on earth, who are and who will be to persevere in the true faith and in penance for otherwise no one will be saved.

With our whole heart, our whole soul, our whole mind, with our whole strength and fortitude, with our whole understanding, with all our powers, with all our efforts, every affection, every feeling, every desire and wish, let us all love the Lord God Who has given and gives to each one of us our whole body, our whole soul and our whole life, Who has created, redeemed, and will save us by His mercy alone, Who did and does everything good for us, miserable and wretched, rotten and foul, ungrateful and evil ones.

Therefore, let us desire nothing else, let us want nothing else, let nothing else please us and cause us delight except our Creator, Redeemer, and Savior, the only true God, Who is the fullness of good, all good, every good, the true and supreme good, Who alone is good, merciful, gentle, delightful and sweet, Who alone is holy, just, true, and upright, Who alone is kind, innocent, clean, from Whom, through Whom and in Whom is all pardon, all grace, all glory of all penitents and just ones, of all the blessed rejoicing together in heaven.

Therefore, let nothing hinder us, nothing separate us, nothing come between us.

Wherever we are, in every place, at every hour, at every time of the day, every day and continually, let all of us truly and humbly believe, hold in our heart and love, honor, adore, serve, praise and bless, glory and exalt, magnify and give thanks to the most High and supreme Eternal God, Trinity and Unity, Father, Son and Holy Spirit, Creator of all, Savior of all, believe and hope in Him, and loves Him. Who, without beginning and end, is unchangeable, invisible, indescribable, ineffable, incomprehensible, unfathomable, blessed, praiseworthy, glorious, exalted, sublime, most high, gentle, lovable, delightful, and totally desirable above all else forever. Amen.

As Christians, we frequently pray the Apostles' Creed. As Catholics, we recite the Nicene Creed when we gather for Sunday Mass. As Franciscans, we have this Franciscan text not only to pray, but also to embrace as a lifestyle which witnesses to our relationship to the Trinity providing us with the foundation for our relationship with one another.

The Word came among us on a mission from heaven to earth, in a movement from the heights to humility and from riches to poverty. St. Bonaventure recognizes in this process a coincidence of opposites: earth leads to heaven, lowliness reaches to the heights, an poverty to wealth. For us, then, earth and heaven are united, the heights and humility are joined, and our poverty becomes our richness. All of this transpires through the Trinity's dwelling within us. We are sent, then, by the Father to continue this work of the Son through the grace of the Holy Spirit. This constitutes our life and our mission.

For Francis of Assisi the Trinity models for us a fraternity-on-mission, that is, brothers and sisters living together in such a way as to preach the Word. Such an involvement in the mystery of the Triune God involves the fraternity in a profound sense of wonder. Josef Pieper, in his monumental work *Leisure: The Basis of Culture,* writes: "Wonder signifies that the world is profounder, more all-embracing and mysterious than the logic of everyday reason had taught us to believe. The innermost meaning of wonder is fulfilled in a deeper sense of mystery. It does not end in doubt but in the awakening of the knowledge that being, as being, is mysterious and inconceivable, and that it is a mystery in the fullest sense of the word ..."[4] Francis would have readily agreed.

St. Francis's *First Letter to the Faithful* ranks among the most basic documents of the early Franciscan movement. In it Francis describes our relationship with God and with one another as a mystical dynamic:

> [We are] spouses, brothers, and mothers of our Lord Jesus Christ. We are spouses when the faithful soul is joined by the Holy Spirit to our Lord Jesus Christ. We are brothers to Him when when we do the will of the Father who is in heaven. We are mothers when we carry Him in our hearts and body through a divine love and a pure and sincere conscience and give birth to Him through a holy activity which much shine as an example before others (1LtF 1:7-10).

---

[4] Josef Pieper, *Leisure: the Basis of Culture* (New York: Pantheon Books, 1964), 101.

This dynamic of the spiritual life weaves us into a Trinitarian tapestry that connects us to one another as we witness to the life of the Trinity, though we fall far short of the exemplar. Likewise, the text has profound implications for the missionary aspect of the Franciscan charism, the mission on which we are sent in the birthing of Jesus in our world, as St. Bonaventure so movingly details in *The Five Feasts of the Child Jesus*. As with any birth, there are pangs as St. Paul so graphically describes: "We know that the whole of creation has been groaning in labor pains until now, and not only the creation, but we ourselves, who have been the first fruits of the Spirit, which we await for adoption, the redemption of our bodies" (Rom 8:22-23). Animated by the spirit of Christ, whom we follow, we humbly accept the invitation to be missionaries.

There may be no better way to contemplate this challenge to be sent as brothers and sisters then to pray with Francis:

> Almighty, eternal, just and merciful God, give us miserable ones, the grace to do for You alone what we know you want us to do and always to desire what pleases you. Inwardly cleansed, interiorly enlightened and inflamed by the fire of the Holy Spirit, may we be able to follow in the footprints of Your beloved Son, our Lord Jesus Christ, and by Your grace alone, may we make our way to You, Most High, Who live and rule in perfect Trinity and simple Unity, and are glorified God almighty forever and ever. Amen (LtOrd 5052).

D. Questions

1. How does Francis's *Letter to the Faithful* challenge me to embrace a Franciscan view of life in relationship with God? Where does it stretch my response?

2. Mission is based upon the life of the Trinity. Mission, for Francis, demanded that he enter into relationships with those to

whom he was sent. How do I enter into relationships with those whom we are sent?

3. How do I contribute my gifts and talents to the communities and/or organizations to which I already belong and in which I participate? How do I affirm, call forth, and develop the gifts and talents of others?

4. Seeing through eyes of wonder, children notice things that adults can no longer perceive. What arouses wonder in my life? Have I lost a sense of wonder? Can I live with and entertain a sense of mystery amid the realities that impinge upon my life?

E. BIBLIOGRAPHY

Johnson, Elizabeth A. *Quest for the Living God: Mapping Frontiers in the Theology of God*. NY: Continuum, 2007. Particularly pp 202-225.
Tarkovsky, Andrei. *Andrei Reblev*. 1966 film. (3 ½ hrs.)
Boff, Leonardo. *Holy Trinity, Perfect Community*. Maryknoll: Orbis, 2000.
Osborne, Kenan B. *The Franciscan Intellectual Tradition: Tracing Its Origins and Identifying Its Central Components*. The Franciscan Heritage Series, vol. I. Pp 53-68. St. Bonaventure: Franciscan Institute, 2003.
Downey, Michael. *Altogether Gift: A Trinitarian Spirituality*. Maryknoll: Orbis, 2000.

F. PICTURE CREDITS

"The Holy Trinity," icon by Andrew Rublev, 1425.

Unit Four

The Gospel Way:
Moving Toward the Reign of God

CONTENTS

From the Franciscan Sources

A.   Introduction

B.   Survey

C.   Information

D.   Questions

E.   Bibliography

F.   Picture Credits

From the Franciscan Sources

He who once enjoyed wearing scarlet robes now traveled about half-clothed. Once while he was singing praises to the Lord in French in a certain forest, thieves suddenly attacked him. When they savagely demanded who he was, the man of God answered confidently and forcefully: "I am the herald of the great King! What is it to you?" They beat him and threw him in the ditch filled with deep snow, saying: "Lie there, you stupid herald of God!" After they left, he rolled about to and fro, shook the snow off himself and jumped out of the ditch. Exhilarated with great joy, he began in a loud voice to make the woods resound with praises to the Creator of all (1C 16).

A. Introduction

It is obvious from the many books, poems and essays as well as paintings and music that continue to be produced about Francis of Assisi, that he has a universal appeal. Perhaps the basis of this appeal is not so much a particular incident in his life or a cause that can be attached to his name as it is his universal perspective. His attitude includes everyone and everything in God's creation. His outlook certainly was *Deus Meus et Omnia*, best rendered "my God and my all," (DBF I:20) for, with God first, he was freely and easily able to relate to all things without possessing them. Francis's frequent use of words like "all" and "every" imply a global, all-embracing outlook. In his *Letter to the Faithful*, he addresses everyone: "Because I am the servant of all, I am obliged to serve all and to administer the fragrant words of the Lord to them" (2LtF 2). In his *Letter to the Rulers of the People*, he writes "to all mayors and consuls, magistrates and governors throughout the world and to all others to whom these words may come" (LtR 1). He also wrote letters to all the guardians of the Brotherhood and even to the entire Order. Then, in his *Canticle of the Sun*, he turns to the entire universe, to all of creation. Francis's view was inclusive, not excluding anyone or anything that is part of God's creation.

B. Survey

While Francis was a man who lived and breathed in Christendom, it did not limit his perspective and therefore his appeal. This is true because, while he was a man of the Church, he was not simply concerned with the Church as an institution. Rather he believed that the Church was the way to a deeper involvement in the Kingdom of God, in which he lived and which he preached by word and example.

In the first part of this unit, we will review Francis's multidimensional understanding of "Church," followed by his commitment to discovering the Kingdom of God in all things. Interestingly enough, his affective relationship with Christ became the foundation for his universal vision.

C. Information

The American theologian, the late Cardinal Avery Dulles became famous for his work, *Models of the Church*, in which he suggests there is not one but several images of the Church, each model providing it with a unique dimension. He articulates five models: the institution, communion, sacrament, servant, and herald. Later he added a sixth model: disciple. Francis would have been comfortable with all of these models.[1]

Francis was committed to the Church as institution with its structures, beliefs, and laws. From his initial call to "Rebuild my house" (which, by Bonaventure's time, had explicitly become "rebuild my Church") to the many disputes among the brothers, he constantly taught his brothers and sisters to adhere to the hierarchical Church in both love and obedience. However, he knew that his call to repair the Church meant that he could

---

[1] Avery Robert Dulles, *Models of the Church* (Garden City: Doubleday, 1974).

not turn a blind eye on what was wrong with the Church. So he was able to see the dangers inherent in any attempt to institutionalize the Gospel: it cannot be solely contained in any structure, especially an institution that had become powerful and rich. His plan for rebuilding, however, was not to condemn the structures but rather to live the Gospel by being powerless and poor within the institution.

There can be no doubt, then, that Francis came to understand the Church as a communion. While he began his journey into God alone, he was soon joined by brothers, whom he considered gifts from God: "The Lord gave me brothers" (Test 14), and by sisters. He lived the Gospel with them, enjoying their company and commitment. This sense of bonding was not naive, as is clear from the story of *Perfect Joy*:

> The same [Brother Leonard] related in the same place that one day at Saint Mary's, blessed Francis called Brother Leo and said: "Brother Leo, write." He responded: "Look, I'm ready!" "Write," he said, "what true joy is."
>
> "A messenger arrives and says that all the Masters of Paris have entered the Order. Write: this isn't true joy! Or, that all the prelates, archbishops and bishops beyond the mountains, as well as the King of France and the King of England [have entered the Order]. Write: this isn't true joy! Again, that my brothers have to the non-believers and converted all of them to the faith; again, that I have so much grace from God that I heal the sick and perform many miracles. I tell you true joy doesn't consist of these things."
>
> "Then what is true joy?"
>
> "I return from Perugia and arrive here in the dead of night. It's winter time, muddy, and so cold that icicles have formed on the edges of my habit and keep striking my legs and blood flows from such wounds. Freezing,

covered with mud and ice, a brother comes and asks: 'Who are you?' 'Brother Francis,' I answer. 'Go away!' he says. 'This is not a decent hour to be wandering about! You may not come in!' When I insist, he replies: 'Go away! You are simple and stupid! Don't come back to us again! There are many of us here like you – we don't need you!' I stand at the door and say: 'For the love of God, take me in tonight!' And he replies: 'I will not! Go to the Crosiers' place and ask there!'

"I tell you this: If I had patience and did not become upset, true joy, as well as true virtue and the salvation of my soul, would consist in this." (True and Perfect Joy 1-15).[2]

Francis truly understood the meaning of communion, for, while it is marked by relationship and intimacy among the members, it can also withstand hurt and rejection, remaining joyfully united to those with whom one is in communion. This insight is particularly important today when followers of the way of St. Francis sometimes necessarily take issue with the institutional Church.

Francis also saw the Church as "the sacrament of encounter with Christ," as the theologian Edward Schillebeeckx phrased it. Francis saw the Church as an instrument through which one is led to the invisible through the visible, to use the phrase made famous by the Victorines.[3] This led Francis to emphasize the Church's sacramental life as is obvious from his two Letters to the Faithful, which are filled with beautiful images and observations about the Eucharist.[4]

And how evident it is that Francis understood the Church as servant! There is probably no other person in the calendar of Saints who took Jesus's call to servanthood more seriously. Time and time again, he refers to himself and his followers

---

[2] *FA:ED* 1, 166-67.
[3] A twelfth century monastic school of mysticism.
[4] 1LtF I:3, 13; 2LtF 6-7, 14-15, 22-24, 33-36, 54-56. Other references to the Eucharist include LtOrd 26-29 and Adm I.

as "servant," "the least of the brethren," and "the little ones." He expected nothing less of the Church, for Jesus said: "The greatest among you will be the one who serves the rest" (Lk. 23:11). Francis's emphasis on being called to serve is no doubt a major aspect of his universal appeal, even though it is a difficult message for the Church and the world.

Who would deny that Francis saw his role in rebuilding the Church by reminding her through example that discipleship is central to Christian life? After all, to be a disciple is to be one who listens to and learns from the Master, who is Jesus (cf. Luke 23:1-12). The liberation theologian Jon Sobrino observes in his *Spirituality of Liberation*: "The call to discipleship is the call to evangelization," that is, the call to live and proclaim the Good News.[5] Thomas of Celano writes of Francis:

> In these last times, a new Evangelist, like one of the rivers of Paradise, has poured out the streams of the gospel in a holy flood over the whole world. He preached the way of the Son of God and the teaching of truth in his deeds. In him and through him an unexpected joy and a holy newness came into the world. A shoot of the ancient religion suddenly renewed the old and decrepit. A new spirit was placed in the hearts of the elect and a holy anointing has been poured out in their midst. This holy servant of God like one of the lights of heaven, shone from above with a new rite and new signs. The ancient miracles have been renewed through him. In the desert of the world a fruitful vine has been planted in a new Order but in an ancient way, bearing flowers, sweet with the fragrance of holy virtues and stretching out everywhere branches of holy religion (1C 89).

This poetic and romantic outburst in the midst of his recounting the story of Francis's life reminds one of the Pauline hymns. Thomas presents Francis as disciple, evangelist and

---

[5] Jon Sobrino, *Spirituality of Liberation: Political Holiness* (Maryknoll: Orbis Books, 1990), 132-33.

servant of the Word of God, whether it is found in print or in hearts, in churches or in creation, in the old or the new.

Yet the more apparent ecclesial image with which Francis identified is that of herald. A herald is one who carries messages to and from his commander. As such the herald was often considered among the *nobilitas minor* (the lesser nobility) not because of his identity but on account of the identity of the one for whom he carries these messages. In his major life of St. Francis, Bonaventure presents Francis as herald on eight different occasions (Prol: 1, 2:5, 4:5, 8:11, 11:3, 12:2, 12:12 and 15:1). However, in none of these references does Bonaventure present Francis as a herald of the Church. Rather he is a herald in the Church who announces the Kingdom of God. Bonaventure, then, broadens the perspective on the herald not only by presenting Francis as "the herald of the great King" (LMj 2:5), but also by emphasizing Francis as "a herald of the Gospel [who] went about the towns and villages proclaiming the kingdom of God not in words taught by human wisdom, but in the power of the Spirit" (LMj 4:5).

Heralds of the Gospel! The *Rules* that Francis and Clare wrote provide Franciscans with a concrete way of gospel living: Francis introduces the *Rule* of 1223 with: "[we are] to observe the holy gospel of our Lord Jesus Christ." Clare's *Rule* repeats the same phrase. An early source gives the first friars their identity in two words: *viri evangelici*—"gospel men" (L3C 51). When asked today about their identity, those inspired by the Franciscan way reply with conviction: "We are a gospel people!" And the gospel proclaims the Kingdom of God.

The Kingdom of God is a very rich scriptural metaphor describing God's loving rule over all creation, and especially God's loving and saving presence in human history. Unlike other kingdoms we study about in world history, the Kingdom of God is not a place, so Jesus says: "The Kingdom of God is among (within) you" (Lk. 17:21). The Kingdom of God is the love of God, boundless and indestructible, filling our hearts with divine love and life. In the imagery of the Irish Dominican poet, Paul

Murray, the love of God is such that "if we were to cease to exist, God would die of grief!" He loves us that much. God sent the Son to bring us that love, which is "poured out in our hearts by the Holy Spirit" (Rom. 5:5). The heart and center of evangelization is the proclamation of that saving love. The purpose of mission is to bring God's loving embrace to the world for the world, as Jesus did as He proclaimed time and again: "The Kingdom of God is here."

The Kingdom arrives in the person of Jesus. As Pope John Paul II says: "The Kingdom of God is not a concept, a doctrine or a program subject to free interpretation. Before all else the Kingdom of God is a person with a face and a name: Jesus of Nazareth, the image of the invisible God."[6]

One of the most memorable speeches of modern times was surely Martin Luther King, Jr.'s "I Have a Dream" speech. Jesus too had a dream: the Kingdom of God. He talks about it more than anything else in the synoptic Gospels. The coming of God's Kingdom was Jesus's passion, the deepest longing of his heart. He invites us to make His desire ours: a passion for the Kingdom of God. The Church, then, is no longer the center of a Christian reality. Rather the Kingdom of God for which Jesus came into the world and which He proclaimed over and over again is the center of this herald's announcement. This is significant since, during Francis's times, the Kingdom and the Church were perceived as identical. In modern times, particularly since the Second Vatican Council, however, an earlier ecclesial tradition has been retrieved, namely that the Church announces and points to the Kingdom of God, which is to be discovered in all creation. The first words of the Dogmatic Constitution on the Church, *Lumen Gentium*, emphasizes this: "Christ is the light of humanity."[7] Paul VI explained: "The Church is not an end unto herself, but rather is fervently concerned to be completely of Christ, in Christ and

---

[6] John Paul II, *Redemptoris missio* (St. Paul Books and Media, 1991).

[7] *Lumen gentium*, *Vatican Council II. The Conciliar and Post Conciliar Documents*, ed. by Austin Flannery, O.P. (Collegeville: Liturgical Press, 1979), 350.

for Christ as well as of men and women, among them and for them."[8]

Given the centrality of the Kingdom motif in the gospel, it is not surprising that this is central to the spirituality of Francis and Clare. In the *Earlier Rule* (ER 23:9), Francis writes: "Let us desire nothing else, let us wish for nothing else. Let nothing else please us or cause us delight, except our Creator and Redeemer and Savior, the one true God, who is the fullness of good, all good, every good, the true and supreme good, who alone is good, who alone is holy, who alone is kind. Therefore let nothing hinder us, nothing separate us or nothing come between us." In his *Rule for Hermitages* (RH3) Francis instructs his friars living in them that their "first concern should be to seek the Reign of God and His justice."

Perhaps Francis's appreciation for the Kingdom of God within all of creation is no more apparent than in his *Canticle of the Sun*:

> Most High, all-powerful, good Lord, Yours are the praises,
> the glory, and the honor, and all blessing,
> To You alone, Most High, do they belong,
> And no human is worthy to mention your name.
>
> Praised be You, my Lord, with all Your creatures,
>   Especially Sir Brother Sun,
>   Who is the day and through whom You give us light.
> And he is beautiful and radiant with great splendor;
>   And bears a likeness of You, Most High One.
> Praised be You, my Lord, through Sister Moon and the stars,
>   In heaven You formed them clear and precious and beautiful.
>
> Praised be You, my Lord, through Brother Wind,

---

[8] Paul VI. "Address at the Opening of the Third Session of Vatican II." *The Pope Speaks*, Vol. 10, No. 2,(1965), 110.

And through the air, cloudy and serene, and every kind of Weather, Through whom You give sustenance to Your creatures.
Praised be You, my Lord, through Sister Water,
Who is very useful and humble and precious and chaste
Praised be You, my Lord, through Brother Fire,
Through whom You light the night, And he is beautiful and playful and robust and strong. Praised be You, my Lord, through our Sister Mother Earth, Who sustains and governs us,
And who produces various fruits with colored flowers and herbs.

Praised be You, my Lord, through those who give pardon for Your love And bear infirmity and tribulation. Blessed are those who endure in peace, For by You, Most High, shall they be crowned.

Praised be You, my Lord, through our Sister Bodily Death,
From whom no one living can escape. Woe to those who die in mortal sin.
Blessed are those whom death will find in Your most holy will, For the second death shall do them no harm.

Praise and bless my Lord and give Him thanks And serve Him with great humility.

Anyone who meditates on this magnificent poem is not reading an ecclesial document or even an explicitly Christian text. Its Christian perspective depends on the faith of the herald of the great King, whose Kingdom can be discovered in the world He created. St. Bonaventure, a passionate mystic who believed and taught that all of creation reveals the Triune God, understood Francis's faith articulated in this canticle. Bonaventure learned from Francis's experience that creation is influenced to its core by the mystery of the ever-present Triune God. This becomes the foundation of his masterpiece, *The Soul's Journey into God*.[9] In lingering over creation, the Christian discovers the Kingdom of God everywhere and so becomes a herald of that Kingdom with Francis.

Like Francis and Clare, those inspired by their charism commit themselves to travel the Gospel way as "pilgrims and strangers," moving towards the Kingdom in the Church. As heralds of the Kingdom that we've discovered, we preach by our love which embraces the world, as Pope John Paul II stated on his visit to Zimbabwe in 1988: "The Church is in the world for the sake of the world!" In other words: For the Kingdom!

D. QUESTIONS

1. How would I describe my vision of the Church? How might I image my vision by painting, drawing, collage, etc.?

2. What is my experience of "church"? In what ways does the Church help me to live my life according to the Gospel? In what ways does the Church make it difficult?

3. Francis writes that the friars first concern "should be to seek the reign of God and God's justice." How does Francis live this out? How does this put him in communion and at odds with the institutional Church? Can I find parallels like this in my life today?

4. Where do I find the "reign of God" most present and active today? What makes visible the invisible for me?

5. What am I a "herald" of? How am I a herald of the Gospel for the people that I interact with on a regular basis?

---

[9] *Itinerarium Mentis in Deum*, VI:2, Philotheus Beohner and Zachary Hayes, eds., WSB II (St. Bonaventure, NY: Franciscan Institute Publications, 2002), 123-25.

E. Bibliography

Carney, Margaret. The First Franciscan Woman: Clare of Assisi & Her Form of Life. Quincy: Franciscan Press, 1993.

Cunningham, Lawrence S. Francis of Assisi: Performing the Gospel Life. Grand Rapids, MI: Eerdmans, 2004.

An Unencumbered Heart: A Tribute to Clare of Assisi 1235-2003. Spirit and Life, 11. Ed. Jean Francois Godet-Calogeras and Roberta McKelvie. St. Bonaventure: Franciscan Institute, 2004.

F. Picture Credits

"Renunciation of Worldly Goods", Scene V, Upper Church, Assisi

Unit Five

The Franciscan Mission

Build With Living Stones

Contents

From the Franciscan Sources

A. Introduction

B. Survey

C. Information

D. Questions

E. Bibliography

F. Picture Credits

From the Franciscan Sources

Francis and his brother Illuminato were led to the Sultan, just as the man of God wished. When the ruler inquired by whom, why and how they had been sent and how they got there, Christ's servant, Francis, answered with an intrepid heart that he had been sent not by man but by the Most High God in order to point out to him and his people the way of salvation and to announce the Gospel of truth. He preached to the Sultan the Triune God and the one Savior of all, Jesus Christ, with such great firmness, such strength of soul, and such fervor of spirit that the words of the Gospel appeared to be truly fulfilled in him: "I will give you utterance and wisdom which all your adversaries will not be able to resist or answer back." The Sultan, perceiving in the man of God a fervor of spirit and a courage that had to be admired, willingly listened to him and invited him to stay longer with him.

A. Introduction

From the beginning Francis of Assisi regarded himself and his followers as missionaries. Indeed Francis discovered his calling on hearing the missionary discourse in the Gospel. After some failed attempts to bring the gospel to the Saracens, Francis went to Egypt in 1219 where he visited the Sultan Melek-al-Kamel. At a time when Pope Innocent III referred to the Muslims as "enemies of Christ and his people" and Mohammed as a "son of perdition," Francis approached the Sultan with the greatest reverence. This well-known visit ushered in a new era of evangelization within the Catholic Church. Francis was the first religious founder to include a separate chapter on the missions in his Rule and he himself was a missionary at home and abroad.[1] In the same year, Francis urged the General

---

[1] Latin *missio*: a sending off + *-arius*: person who. See *Random House Webster's College Dictionary* (New York: Random House, Inc., 1995), 79, 867.

Chapter of the Order to agree on a program of evangelization for the non-Christian world. Francis offered his followers a way to "live spiritually among the Saracens and nonbelievers," (ER 16:5) commonly referred to as The Missionary Mandate.

B. Survey

Before the Second Vatican Council, we frequently spoke of "having missions." The Council shifted such thinking by stating that "the Church is missionary by its very nature." In our study of the Trinity, we saw the reason for this in the fact that "the Church takes her origin from the mission of the Son and the mission of the Holy Spirit."[2] Our Church is a missionary Church because our God is a missionary God. The Father sends the Son, The Son sends the Holy Spirit and the Spirit sends the whole Church—the People of God—into the world on mission. It is imperative, then, that each baptized Christian accept his or her role as a missionary and that we, who desire to be missionaries with a Franciscan outlook, understand Francis's unique contribution to the meaning of being sent into the world.

There are any number of historical and contemporary documents from all branches of the Franciscan Order that explicate this unique meaning of being missionaries. All the themes contained in them, however, are seminally contained in the two documents we will study in some depth: The Missionary Mandate of Francis of Assisi contained in Chapter 16 of the Earlier Rule and Pope Paul VI's revolutionary apostolic exhortation *Evangelii Nuntiandi* (Proclaimers of the Gospels), which has not only formed much contemporary thought on mission but has also been the basis of Pope John Paul Is call for a "new evangelization."

---

[2] *Ad Gentes Divinitus*, #3-5: The Decree on the Church's Missionary Activity. *Vatican Council II: The Conciliar and Post Concilim Documents* (Collegeville: Liturgical Press, 1975), 814-18.

C. Information

Francis's view of mission can be understood only within the framework of his own time and his particularly unique vision. The encounter with lepers had revealed to Francis a new evangelical vision of the universal fraternity of all creatures. All men and women without exception belonged to this sacred fraternity. This was the "form of life" which Francis felt called to share with the world. To live in this manner was to live in penance, affirming everything that strengthened the bonds of the human fraternity and repenting of all that did not. And because this is what it meant to do penance, this is also the primary content of the friars' penitential preaching, both at home as well as abroad. Franciscan mission is all about sharing this vision of life.

In 1212, six years after his conversion, Francis and a few companions attempted to travel to Syria "to preach the Christian faith and penance" (1C 55) to the Saracens (terms used to refer to Muslims in the East). However, his ship encountered a storm that resulted in it being diverted to the Dalmatian coast (cf. 1C 55). So he was forced to return home. He tried again the following year, this time travelling West to Spain in order to reach the miramolin of Morocco. But this time illness forced him to once again abandon his goal.

Francis never gave up his idea of preaching to the Saracens, however. At the Pentecost Chapter of 1219, he broached the idea of sending the brothers to Tunisia and Morocco. Francis went to Egypt, as is evidenced from our story From the Franciscan Sources at the beginning of this unit. Thus he not only issued a mandate but also set an example.

The Missionary Mandate of St. Francis (ER16) deserves to be studied prayerfully by us to learn to appreciate Francis's call and example.

The Lord says: "Behold I am sending you like sheep in the midst of wolves." Therefore, "Be prudent as serpents and simple as doves." Let any brother, then, who desires by divine inspiration *to go among the Saracens and other nonbelievers, go with the permission of his minister and servant. If he sees that they are fit to be sent, the minister may give them permission and not oppose them, for he will be bound to render an accounting to the Lord if he has proceeded without discernment in this and other matters.*

Francis's encounter with the sultan, Malek al-Kamil, is one of the most imporant and instructive events in the life of the Poverello. Adopting an attitude of respect and dialogue, rather than self-righteousness and vehemence, he and his companion, Illuminato, by all accounts engaged in a sharing of faith with the sultan and his court, each presenting his belief in the one God from his own perspective. How different the approach – and the end-result – of the five friars who had gone to Morocco in the same year! Indeed, it would appear that their aggressive proselytizing and consequent beheadings in January 1220 profoundly dismayed Francis. Historians now believe that in reaction to the outcome of the mission to Morocco, Francis added a new chapter to the Early Rule, Chapter 16, which outlines a profoundly respectful – a uniquely Franciscan – approach to mission among the non-believers.

Francis immediately situates our mission by starting Chapter 16 with the words "The Lord says ..." The motivation for the Franciscan missionary must be founded and grounded in a Gospel vision: the good news for a world that has lost its way. Francis takes his lead from this good news rather than from the dominant culture of his day, not even the dominant ecclesiastical culture of his day.

It is extremely difficult, if not impossible, for us not to be affected by the cultures in which we live and move. Yet we must work to see, act and judge our surroundings by the Word of God in such a way that we allow this Word to illuminate our human, cultural experiences, helping us to make moral and spiritual judgments from a Gospel perspective.

As Paul VI said: "The Church exists to evangelize; that is our deepest identity."[3] Since we are the Church, we are called to

---

[3] Paul IV, *Evangelii Nutiandi*, #14 (Washington: Publications Office, United States Catholic Conference, 1976).

evangelize by making this Gospel perspective the source of our mission.

As for the brothers who go, they can live spiritually among the Saracens and nonbelievers in two ways. One way is not to engage in arguments and disputes but to be subject "to every human creature for God's sake" and to acknowledge that they are Christians. The other way is to announce the Word of God, when they see it pleases the Lord, in order that unbelievers may believe in almighty God, the Father, the Son and the Holy Spirit, the Creator of all, the Son, the Redeemer and Savior, and be baptized and become Christians because 'no one can enter the kingdom of God without being reborn of water and the Holy Spirit.

The first way that Francis proposes is indeed revolutionary. This can readily be seen when one compares Francis's sentiments with those of Pope Innocent III expressed at the Fourth Lateran Council: "We excommunicate the false Christians who provide supplies for the Saracens ... and those who serve them." This Council also repeated the declarations of former councils which forbad Christians to be of service to Jews or other nonchristians. For Francis, the important thing was that his followers would go among people not only as brothers and sisters but as lesser brothers and sisters, in a spirit of service. So he instructs his followers that, when staying with others, they "should not be administrators or managers, but lesser ones subject to all who are in the same house" (ER VII: Iff).

This way of being in the world is a call to true Christian humility in the sense of not acting arrogantly as "possessors" of the Word of God that would permit us to foist the truth upon others. It would be well to recall the words of William Sloan Coffin that too many Christians use the Bible like a drunk uses a light post: not for enlightenment but for support. The Word of God should not be used by us to support our insecurities but to enlighten the darkness of our minds and hearts along with the dimness of the world.

Even Francis's second way of being sent into the world is revolutionary, for his call to announce the Gospel presupposes that we are living the Gospel: we proclaim what we are experiencing. Again Paul VI takes up this theme when he reminds us that" ... in the Church the witness given by a life truly and essentially Christian which is dedicated to God in an indissoluble union and which is likewise dedicated with the utmost fervor of soul to our neighbor is the primary organ of evangelization. As we said recently in an address to a group of laypersons: 'the people of our day are more impressed by witnesses than by teachers, and if they listen to these it is because they also bear witness'."[4]

Even Francis's approach to preaching differed substantially from the preaching of his times. The Dominicans preached against heresy; the Benedictines expounded on the glories of the liturgy; and St. Francis advised that his followers "preach for the benefit and edification of the people, announcing to them vices and virtues, punishment and glory, with brevity, because the Lord when on earth kept his word brief" (LR 9:3).

They can say to them and to the others these and other things which please God because the Lord says in the Gospel: "Whoever acknowledges me before others I will acknowledge before my heavenly Father. Whoever is ashamed of me and of my words, the Son of Man will be ashamed of when he comes in his glory and in the glory of the Father."

Francis was aware of the reality that his early followers, like his present day followers, may be hesitant about acknowledging their faith to a non-believing world. He therefore reminds us of our obligations to acknowledge our faith, not as television evangelists shouting loudly and gesturing wildly, but rather calmly and contemplatively being who we say we are.

Once again we are reminded of the very solid advice of Paul VI: "Young people in particular are said to have a horror of falsity and hypocrisy and to seek above all truth and clarity. These 'signs of the times' should convince us of the necessity of the utmost vigilance. We are continually being questioned, sometimes tacitly, sometimes openly: Do you believe yourself what you are

---

[4] Paul VI, #41.

saying to us? Is your life in accord with your beliefs? Is your preaching in accord with your life?"[5] If our lives remain silent, no one will hear the Gospel today.

> *Wherever they may be, let all the brothers remember that they have given themselves and abandoned their bodies to the Lord Jesus Christ. For love of Him, they must make themselves vulnerable to their enemies, both visible and invisible, because the Lord says: "Whoever loses his life because of me will save it" in eternal life. "Blessed are they who suffer persecution for the sake of justice, for theirs is the kingdom of heaven. If they have persecuted me, they will also persecute you. If they persecute you in one town, flee to another. Blessed are you when people hate you, speak evil of you, persecute, expel, and abuse you, denounce your name as evil and utter every kind of slander against you because of me. Rejoice and be glad on that day because your reward is great in heaven. I tell you, my friends, do not be afraid of them and do not fear those who kill the body and afterwards have nothing more to do. See that you are not alarmed. For by your patience, you will possess your souls; whoever perseveres to the end will be saved."*

This may be called a third way of "living spiritually among" non-christians: proclaiming the Gospel by patiently suffering persecution and martyrdom. Mission can cost life and limb. The early followers of Francis were willing to embrace martyrdom. Such a stance rarely became a reality because people do not normally kill those who want to live peacefully and humbly among them, seeking only to be subject to all. However, we do know that the first martyrs from the Franciscan Order in Morocco did not let themselves be guided by Francis's vision of "living among." The peaceful co-existence of Christians and Muslims was evident until the imprudent behavior of the brothers destroyed it. They engaged in polemics against the Muslims and it reached a point where it became too much even for the Christians residing there. They then sent the brothers home in a ship. But they returned and continued their polemics. On account of this, in ac-

---

[5] Paul IV, #76.

cord with Islamic law, the Muslims beheaded them for preaching against the Prophet.

Recent studies on Clare of Assisi reveal that she too thought of going on a mission to die a martyr. She wanted to leave the seclusion of San Damiano and follow the example of the five martyrs of Morocco. This dramatic moment in the life of Clare is affirmed in the files of her canonization process: "Lady Clare was in such fire of spirit that, for the sake of her love of God, she wanted to die a martyr. That was evident when she learned that some brothers in Morocco had been tortured, and she expressed her intention to go there herself" (Proc 6:6). Another witness gave her testimony: "She wanted to die a martyr for the sake of her love for God, in order to defend her faith and her religious order. Before she fell ill, she wished to go to Morocco, the place where, as one says, the brothers had died as martyrs" (Proc. 7:2).

In a poetic moment, Thomas of Celano says that Francis "filled the whole world with the Gospel of Christ" (1C 97). This is our ongoing missionary task, perhaps best expressed in the haunting story of Francis and the sinful people of Poggio Bustone, who were in serious need of conversion. Rather than condemn them, Francis regularly emerged from his hermitage in the hills to greet the people of the town, simply calling out: Buon giorno, Buona gente—Good Morning, good people—until they came to believe it and were converted.

D. QUESTIONS

1. As Francis met the Sultan with respect and openness, how am I called today to behaviors of presence, dialogue, and acceptance to others?

2. How do I understand myself as being sent on a mission? How do I participate in the missionary aspect of the Church?

3. What does the term "new evangelization" mean to me? How do I participate in the missionary aspect of the Church?

4. What aspects of the American culture today need to be evangelized? What approaches might be utilized to bring the Gospel message to these aspects?

5. How do I witness to my belief while respecting the diversity of and/or the lack of religious sentiments present in American culture today?

6. What can Franciscans and their wisdom around mission offer as a witness in our world and Church today?

E. FURTHER READING

Hoeberichts, Jan. *Francis and Islam*. Quincy: Franciscan Press, 2004.

Moses, Paul. *The Saint and the Sultan: The Crusades, Islam, and Francis of Assisi's Mission of Peace*. New York: Doubleday, 2009.

Tolan, John. *Saint Francis and the Sultan: The Curious History of a Christian-Muslim Encounter*. New York: Oxford. 2009.

Dardess, George and Marvin Mich. *In the Spirit of St. Francis and the Sultan: Muslims and Catholics Working Together for the Common Good*. Maryknoll: Orbis. 2011.

Daring to Embrace the Other: Franciscans and Muslims in Dialogue (2008) Mitchell, Daria, ed. Spirit and Life 12. St. Bonaventure: Franciscan Institute. 2009.

Mirroring One Another, Reflecting the Divine: The Franciscan-Muslim Journey Into God. Mitchell, Daria, ed. Spirit and Life 13. St. Bonaventure: Franciscan Institute. 2009

F. PICTURE CREDITS

Santa Croce: Bardi Chapel Trial by Fire, St. Francis Before the Sultan

Unit Six

To be Formed into Christ Jesus

Contents

From the Franciscan Sources

A. Introduction

B. Survey

C. Information

D. Questions

E. Bibliography

F. Picture Credits

From the Franciscan Sources

One day, while he was riding on horseback through the plain that lies below the town of Assisi, he came upon a leper. This unforeseen encounter struck him with horror. But he recalled his resolution to be perfect and remembered that he must first conquer himself if he wanted to become a knight of Christ. He slipped off his horse and ran to kiss the man. When the leper put out his hand as if to receive some alms, Francis gave him his money and a kiss. Immediately mounting his horse, Francis looked all around; but although the open plain stretched clear in all directions, he could not see the leper anywhere. Filled with wonder and joy, he began devoutly to sing God's praises, resolving from this always to strive to do greater things in the future. From that time on he clothed himself with the spirit of poverty, a sense of humility and a feeling of intimate devotion. Formerly he used to be horrified not only by close dealing with lepers but by their very sight, even from a distance; but now he rendered humble service to the lepers with human concern and devoted kindness. He visited their houses frequently, generously distributed alms to them and with great compassion kissed their hands and their mouths (LMj 1:4-5).

A. Introduction

Those who are sent on mission need an adequate formation. Today it is the accepted norm for us to learn the language and study the culture in which we live and work. Such familiarity leads to a deeper appreciation of that culture and more effective service. But Franciscan formation requires far more than this since a person desiring to live the Gospel in the Franciscan Tradition must also want to be formed into Christ Jesus. This is obvious from the clothes motif in the early chapters of St. Bonaventure's, *Major Life of St. Francis*. In this work Francis is presented as taking off and putting on clothing until he finally realizes his call to put on Christ Jesus.

Our subject in this unit, then, is Franciscan preparation for mission. We need to remember that Francis did not make a sharp distinction between being on mission at home and abroad, in a supposedly Christian environment and a non-Christian one. In either situation the goal is identical: to bear witness to the kingdom of God by living the Gospel. We are formed into Christ Jesus for the sake of our world.

B. Survey

It is evident from the *Testament* of St. Francis that the experience of embracing the leper was more than a one-time event. The embrace of the leper was a formative moment that changed the way he lived and where he lived. Later, when brothers came to join him, he sent them to be formed among the lepers, just as he was formed by them. As years passed, this experience was replaced by their followers' close contact with Francis and Clare. They became the formators by example and exhortation for those who desired to live from this new evangelical perspective.

C. Information

The embrace of the leper by St. Francis has become one of the most telling images of his life. Giotto recounts it in art; all of Francis's biographers retell it. The danger is that we see this experience as a single event that is both memorable and challenging rather than as a formative experience that changed Francis's way of life. Francis did not simply kiss one leper; he also cared for lepers, bandaged them, and, most importantly, lived among them as a lesser brother.

The significance of this experience is evident from Francis's own words: "The Lord gave me, Brother Francis, thus to begin doing penance in this way: for when I was in sin, it seemed too bitter for me to see lepers. And the Lord Himself led me among them and I showed mercy to them. And when I left them, what had seemed bitter to me was turned into sweetness of soul and body. And afterwards I delayed a little and left the world" (Test 1-3).[1]

Perhaps the impact upon Francis of embracing the leper is even more telling. This can be seen from his desire that those entering the fraternity serve the lepers: "They must rejoice when they live among people of little value and looked down upon, among the poor and the powerless, the sick and the lepers, and the beggars by the wayside " (ER 9:2). In *The Mirror of Perfection* we read: "He wished the friars to live in leper-houses to serve them, and by doing so to establish themselves in holy humility. For whenever anyone, whether noble or commoner, entered the Order, among the other instructions given him, he was told that he must humbly serve the lepers and live with them in their houses" (2MP 44). Living among the lepers and serving them seems to be the first responsible task of the early followers of Francis, probably even their earliest residences. Pope Gregory IX was aware of this and even attempted to follow Francis's admonition. St. Bonaventure reminds us of this in a sermon of 1267: "[the Pope], who was a man full of wisdom, because of his great friendship with St. Francis, followed his example closely. He kept a leper in his room and, dressed in the habit of a friar, looked after him. One day the leper said to him: 'Has the Supreme Pontiff no one but an old man like you, to look after me?'" [2]

Very early on, however, the image of the leper as formator was replaced by the image of Francis himself as the *forma minorum* ("model of the minors"). Surely one of the purposes of St. Bonaventure's *Major Life of St. Francis* was to provide the followers of Francis with a form to shape their individual lives, a mentor to imitate. Such a development was neither unexpected nor undesirable, though we need to be ever aware of Francis's own regret near the end of his life: "He burned with a great desire to return to his earliest steps toward humility; rejoicing in hope because of his boundless love, he planned to call his body back to its original servitude.... He wanted to return to serving lepers and to be held in contempt, just as he used to be"

---
[1] *FA:ED* 1, 124.
[2] *FA:ED* 2, 751.

(1C 103). We recall that Francis often referred to people with leprosy as brother and sister Christians (cf. LP 22).

Several issues concerning our formation into Christ Jesus arise from these accounts.

First, and perhaps most importantly, is the inescapable principle that people not programs form the Franciscan person. Programs are certainly necessary for they provide the necessary structures for a person to progress through a formative process. But, just as Francis was formed by his encounters with lepers, so too anyone who desires to think and feel as a follower of the Poverello, must look to persons for guidance.

Perhaps the Inter-Franciscan Mission Congress held at Mattli, Switzerland (1982), formulated this best:

> We observe that the Church and the world are changing rapidly. There is a danger that traditional ideas and models will not adequately provide a continual process of learning and ongoing formation.
>
> We recall that Francis of Assisi was always open to the signs of his times. He did not confront situations with preconceived notions. He was always prepared to learn, even from the newest novice. He wished formation to be done, not primarily at universities but in leper colonies. He was convinced that a [Franciscan-oriented person] could not understand what [one] had not experienced.
>
> Even theological education should first of all concern itself with personal conversion and then the proclamation of the Gospel. Therefore, we wish to learn from one another, as sisters and brothers, above all by sharing experiences, by reading the gospel, by praying together, by breaking the bread of the Eucharist together, and by evaluating our roles in this process.

We Franciscans take seriously the words of Gregory the Great: "The poor are our teachers, the humble our learned ones.³

This statement provides us with a guide in developing some characteristics for a program that will assist individuals to be formed into Christ Jesus for the sake of the Kingdom.

The first requirement is for the community to identify itself as a group of learners. We can no longer presume to have the answers to the many Franciscan questions that have confronted us throughout our history and still plague us today. Because the questions were answered differently, there is much diversity within the Franciscan Movement. This diversity, while historically painful, has given the Movement its appeal along with its respect for the individual. Franciscans are people who have found their own identity through Francis and Clare. This is an ongoing process of discovery that takes place within the community of learners, who remain open to grace-filled encounters and conversions.

This group of learners must realize that they are simultaneously teachers and pupils. In other words, the formative Franciscan experience is horizontal rather than vertical, circular rather than hierarchical. Another word for learning within the Franciscan Tradition, then, is *listening*.

Francis listened to everything and everyone. He claimed no infallible knowledge of what to do. Rather, this was given to him, revealed to him, and he responded. All of his life he was a learner who listened intently to the Lord, his brothers and sisters, and to each individual, even the youngest among them (cf. 2C 151).

The same attitude can be found in the relationships of St. Clare. She states in her Rule that the abbess is to consult with all her sisters about all those things which concern the welfare and the good of the monastery, for "the Lord often reveals what is best to the lesser among us "(RC114:13)

---

³ "The Inter-Franciscan Message, Mattli, Switzerland, 1982." *Franciscan Missionary Charism in Contemporary Franciscan and Church Documents* (Quezon City: CCFMC Office, 1986), 231.

So, while there are teachers and pupils as well as formators and those to be formed among us, our primary identity is that of brothers and sisters. However, St. Bonaventure reminds us in his first sermon on St. Francis (1255) (*FA:ED* 2, 512): "To arrive at knowledge without a human teacher is not for everyone, but the privilege of a few. Though the Lord Himself chose to teach St. Paul and St. Francis, it is His will that their disciples be taught by human teachers." And wasn't even Francis taught by the leper? And the young novice? And all those to whom he so intently listened?

The learning within the group fundamentally arises from the experiences of the individuals within the group, founded on the firm belief that these are grace-filled and grace-revealing experiences. Knowledge is important and must be shared but wisdom is arrived at when knowledge and understanding are related through experience. The poet Wallace Stevens very well expresses this, when he writes in Notes *from a Sublime Fiction*:

> Perhaps
> The truth depends on a walk around a lake,
> A composing as the body tires, a stop
> To see hepatica, to stop to watch
> A certain definition grow certain and
> A wait within that certainty, a rest
> In the swags of pine-trees bordering the lake.[4]

In the same work, he refers to "the academies like structures in the mist." Experience leads us from the mist into the sunlight, to the experience of illumination, by so engaging us that we become disciples, listening for the divine in the all too human or even the seemingly subhuman circumstances of daily life.

The corollary of this is that the wider the range of experience within the developing Franciscan community, the greater is potential for growth. The very varieties of these faith experiences are a key to understanding the role of a Franciscan-oriented person on mission.

---

[4] Wallace Stevens, "Notes Toward a Supreme Fiction," *Wallace Stevens: Collected Poetry and Prose* (New York: Library of America, Literary Classics of the U.S. Inc., 1997), 333-34.

This aim is accomplished by the reading of the scriptures together. The one indispensable textbook for people who desire to have a Franciscan perspective on life is the Gospel, upon which Francis calls us to base our lives. We judge our experiences in the light of the Word of God. Such a communal celebration of the Word can lead us to an evangelical intuition into the meaning of life and the world in which we live.

Prayer is an essential part of being formed into Christ Jesus. It nourishes faith, strengthens values, deepens insight, and promotes sensitivity to constantly rediscover our mission. Prayer and mission go hand-in-hand as is obvious from Bonaventure's account of Francis's encounter with the leper. It was fundamentally a prayerful experience.

An important aspect of Franciscan prayer is sanctifying the day through praying the Liturgy of the Hours.[5] Peggy Rosenthal, in her work *The Poets' Jesus*, reflects: "If seven times a day, you chant the psalms and hear a passage from Scripture, the rhythm of that enormous range of human emotion taken up into prayer inevitably seeps into your whole being."[6] Perhaps that is why Francis was insistent upon his followers praying the hours and making them their own, as he did in the *Office of the Passion*.[7]

A privileged way in which we pray together is at the celebration of the Eucharist (Mass). The Eucharist (also called the Mass) is an unbloody rerepresentation of Christ's sacrifice on Calvary and the gift of himself in the forms of bread and wine at the Last Supper. The word *Eucharist* is Greek for "thanksgiving," i.e., that which is continually offered to the Father by Christ (in the person of the priest) through the power of the Holy Spirit. This prayer builds up our life together by uniting us more closely

---

[5] The Liturgy of the Hours (formerly, the Divine Office) is the Church's public prayer of praise and thanksgiving, prayed in Christ's name and in union with the saints and angels in heaven. Eight timeframes each day are sanctified by one of the "Hours," which are prayed by ordained clergy, consecrated men and women and many lay people, usually in public, but also in private settings. These prayers include psalms; readings from scripture, the Fathers and lives or writings of the saints; hymns; intercessory prayers, and concluding prayers.

[6] Peggy Rosenthal, *The Poet's Jesus* (New York: Oxford University Press, 2000), 145.

[7] *FA:ED* 1, 140-57.

to Christ, who joins us as brothers and sisters. We must also become aware of and committed to the social implications of the Eucharist. The lepers in our lives, including the leper within, cannot be excluded from our celebration and our life, for it is the leper who reveals to us how truly poor we are: everything good we are and have comes from the goodness of God.[8] So the poor become our teachers in discovering our own poverty, the authenticity with which we must live, and the humility that is necessary to accept life as it is.

There are any number of models for being formed into a Franciscan person with a mission, many based upon a variety of models of the Church. Among the most popular among Franciscans are:

> • The Personalist Model places the emphasis on the individual being formed rather than upon the mission for which one is called. Formation takes place "where the person is at" so that there is very little structure and often enough very little guidance. While this model is very appealing to Franciscans, its biggest problem is that it is self-centered rather than Christ-centered. One is reminded that, when Brother Leo was suffering an inner struggle, Francis did not center upon him and his issues but rather refocused Leo with *The Praises of God*.

> • The Rite of Christian Initiation of Adults Model is an ecclesial model that provides a process, a communal approach involving everyone within the community, involves a deepening sense of belonging, and shares the stories of faith. There is much richness in this model for Franciscans, especially its emphasis on togetherness, storytelling, and commitment. The difficulty for Franciscans is that it is primarily oriented toward the Church rather than the Kingdom.

> • The Pilgrim Model is particularly appealing to those attracted to the way of Francis and Clare since Francis

---

[8] *Praises of God, FA:ED* 1, 109.

insisted upon our looking at this life "as pilgrims and strangers." For those on pilgrimage, there is a release from everyday structures, simplicity of dress and behavior allowing for easy mobility, and movement toward the experience of the sacred. Further, it creates a new understanding of community where relationships are more spontaneous, normative, and non-hierarchical.

• The Disciple Model is an evangelical model based upon a personal relationship with Christ in a listening stance that leads to new and deeper relationships. In a sense, it is a combination of the personalist model (though the person is Christ, who teaches us what it means to be a person) and the pilgrim model (though one travels the road of the Gospel rather than being a world traveler).

Whatever model is chosen, it is imperative that our formation into persons being sent into the world for the sake of the Kingdom centers upon being formed into Christ Jesus, who is ultimately discovered in the formation mentor, whether that is the one with leprosy, an AIDS patient, an elderly person, or even the teacher.

D. QUESTIONS

1. Who are the lepers in the world/in my life today? What have I learned from them? How do they teach me?

2. Do I often reflect on my daily experiences? How open am I to receive new truths/insights that may be encountered there?

3. Who have been models/formators of Christian living for me? How have I incorporated their virtues into my life? Recall an incident involving that person that was especially memorable and significant. What are some ways in which my life invites others to believe the good news?

4. Where do I need to be more Christ-like in my life? What qualities/virtues am I seeking to develop?

5. What practices, e.g. reading the Bible, personal/communal prayer, serving the poor, infirm, elderly, spiritual direction, etc. do I need to incorporate into my life to help me grow in my Christian identity?

E. BIBLIOGRAPHY

Brunette, Pierre. *Francis of Assisi and His Conversions.* Quincy: Franciscan Press, 1997.

Nguyen-Van-Khanh, Norbert. *The Teacher of His Heart: Jesus Christ in the Thought and Writings of St. Francis.* St. Bonaventure: Franciscan Institute, 1994.

E PICTURE CREDITS

Stigmatization of St. Francis, Scene XIX, Upper Church, Assisi

UNIT SEVEN

THE FRANCISCAN EVANGELIST:
DEVELOPING A CONTEMPLATIVE CONSCIOUSNESS

Contents

From the Franciscan Sources

A. Introduction

B. Survey

C. Information

D. Questions

E. Bibliography

F. Picture Credits

From the Franciscan Sources

Francis turned all his time into a holy leisure in which to engrave wisdom on his heart, so that, if he did not always advance, he would not seem to give up. If visits from people of the world or any kind of business intruded, he would cut them short rather than finish with them, and hurry back to the things that are within. The world had no flavor for him, fed on the sweetness of heaven, and divine delicacies had spoiled him for crude human fare. He always sought out a hidden place where he could join to God not only his spirit but every member of his body. When it happened that he was suddenly overcome in public by a visitation of the Lord, so as not to be without a cell, he would make a little cell out of his mantle. Sometimes, when he had no mantle, he would cover his face with his sleeve to avoid revealing his hidden manna. Indeed, in order to make all the marrow of his heart a holocaust in manifold ways, he would place before his eye the One who is manifold and supremely simple. He would often ruminate inwardly with unmoving lips, and drawing outward things inward, he raised his spirit to the heights. Thus he would direct all his attention and affection toward the one thing he asked of the Lord, not so much praying as becoming a prayer. How deeply would you think he was pervaded with sweetness as he grew accustomed to such things? He knows. I can only wonder. Those with experience will be given this knowledge; but it is not granted to those with no experience (2C 61).

A. Introduction

Putting aside the dualistic attitude toward the body and the world for the moment and reflecting upon the many beautiful images of prayer in this brief excerpt from Thomas of Celano's reflections, we can come to a definition of Franciscan prayer: it is not so much saying prayers as it is becoming a prayer. Francis was devoured by two desires: to live the Gospel, a desire which assumed both being among the people and spending time apart from them, as well as the desire to be absorbed into Christ Jesus. Prayer was never an escape from contact with others, for it was with his brothers and sisters that he was able to live and experience the Gospel. But it was his relationship with Jesus that became the foundation of all his other relationships. Such an attitude required Francis to be absorbed into the presence of God even in the midst of life's demands and distractions. It was this contemplative consciousness that led Francis to opt "to live for Him who died for all" (1C 35). Thus Francis wanted to be as present to Jesus as Jesus was to him and to die for all his brothers and sisters, so he gave his life for the sake of the preaching of Gospel. Turning to God and turning to the world were not separated in his life. He believed that one can encounter God wherever one is, provided God is the source of one's life.

B. Survey

The Word of God absorbed both Francis and Clare so that they became more and more identified with Christ. This experience was fulfilled for Francis through the imprint of the Stigmata of Jesus upon his body and for Clare through her transfiguration into the light of Christ for her sisters, as her name so appropriately signifies. Clare would have been very comfortable with the poet Mary Oliver's description of prayer in *Winter Hours* as "a dipping of oneself toward the light."[1]

C. Information

Francis of Assisi was a contemplative who possessed "the Spirit of the Lord and His holy manner of working" (LR 10:8). For Francis, to contemplate was to linger over an experience to discover the presence of God in that experience as did Augustine in his Confessions and as did Francis himself in his *Testament*. Such contemplative moments led to a contemplative

---

[1] Mary Oliver, *Winter Hours* (Boston: Houghton Mifflin Harcourt, 1999), 107.

consciousness, which developed within Francis so that he became aware of God's presence at the very moment of any experience. Beauty is an essential aspect of Franciscan contemplation, as we shall see particularly from Clare. But beauty is not discovered; it strikes one. To be struck by the beautiful, one must develop an eye for it, an ability to recognize it during the experience of seeing it. One must be alert. This is contemplative consciousness through which one will even discover the beauty of the leper in the midst of the experience.

Francis and Clare possessed this contemplative consciousness, so that there were not only contemplative moments in their lives but they themselves became prayers. Dichotomies disappeared. Whether in prayer or on mission, their lives were prayers rising to the Father through the Son with the assistance of the Holy Spirit.

The prayers of Francis are not so much prayers of petition, then, as they are prayers of thanksgiving because Francis did not approach God as a problem-solver but rather as a gift-giver toward whom he should be grateful. When Francis speaks of God, his language suddenly changes from a helpless scribbler to a literary giant. The words flow articulately and poetically. Many of these writings are pure prayer, expressive hymns, prefaces, litanies, and chants. Francis shared his experience of God through words, gestures, and even music so that his followers could go about the world praising God and encouraging others to join in this praise. This is evident not only in the prayers themselves but also in Chapter 22 of the *Earlier Rule*, where Francis provides his brothers with a vision for their missionary endeavors, which he had already expounded upon in Chapter 16 of the same *Rule* (cf. Unit 5). This vision is perhaps Francis's best explanation of how he believes his followers should become living prayers.

Alluding to Jesus's parable of the seed falling on rocky ground, Francis says: "Let us be careful that we are not earth along the wayside, or that which is rocky or full of thorns, in keeping with what the Lord says in the Gospel: 'the word of God is a seed.'" Thus Francis establishes reception of the Word of God as the foundation for Franciscan prayer. Prayer is the gift of the Word in our hearts. But receptivity to the Word is not enough. The Word that is conceived within us is to be born into the world through our preaching. For Francis, there was no dichotomy between preaching and praying because one really cannot have one without the other. The Word that is given as a gift must be passed on as a gift. Surely Paul reflects this sentiment when he exclaims: "I cannot not preach the gospel." It becomes a magnificent obsession, one that Francis shared. Most assuredly Francis would agree with the observation of Abraham Joshua Heschel in his work *Quest for God*, when he writes: "Preach in order to pray. Preach in order to inspire others to pray. The test of a true sermon is that it can be converted to prayer."[2]

This penchant for turning from self-centeredness to God-centeredness is also evident in the litany that Francis gave to Leo who was seemingly depressed and feeling quite inferior to the other brothers. When Leo asked for Francis's help, Francis did not focus on Leo's problems but rather re-focused Leo with this beautiful *Praises of God*:

> You are the holy Lord God Who does wonderful things.
>
> You are strong, You are great. You are the most high.
>   You are almighty king. You are holy Father, King of heaven and earth.
>
> You are three and one, the Lord God of gods;
>   You are the good, all good, the highest good, Lord God living and true.
>
> You are love, charity; You are wisdom, You are humility,
>   You are patience, You are beauty, You are meekness,
> You are security, You are rest,
>   You are gladness and joy, You are our hope, You are justice, You are moderation, You are all our riches to sufficiency.

---

[2] Elaine Scarry, *On Beauty and Being Just* (Princeton: Princeton University Press, 2000), 51.

You are beauty, you are meekness,
> You are the protector, You are our custodian and defender,
> You are strength, You are refreshment. You are our hope, You are our faith, You are our charity,
> You are all our sweetness, You are our eternal life:
> Great and wonderful Lord, Almighty God, Merciful Savior.[3]

This touchingly pastoral text re-orients Leo away from his concerns and problems to the very gift who is God.

In recasting the life of St. Francis, St. Bonaventure presents Francis's identification with Christ in the Stigmata as a model for the Franciscan person desirous of becoming a prayer. As Chapter 10 progresses, Bonaventure leads the reader through an illuminative process that presents prayer as a loving encounter between the disciple and Master, the lover and the Beloved. This relationship, guided by the Holy Spirit, possesses certain qualities that will help the reader to evaluate the state of this ongoing and developing relationship, not only with God but also with others through the God. Such qualities could be described as 'qualities of Franciscan prayer.'"

According to St. Bonaventure, the first quality of this affectionate understanding of prayer is that it results in a holy forgetfulness. The lover is so enamored of the Beloved that the focus of attention, affection, and even obsession is on the Other:

> For instance, one time when he was traveling through Borgo San Sepolcro, a heavily populated town, and was riding on a donkey because of physical weakness, crowds rushed to meet him out of devotion. He was touched by them, pulled and shoved by them, yet he seemed not to feel any of this, and as if he were a lifeless corpse, did not notice what was going on around him. Long after he had passed the town and left the crowds, he came to a dwelling of lepers, and the contemplator of heaven, as if

---

[3] "Praises of God," *Francis of Assisi: Early Documents* (New York: New City Press, 1999), 1, 109.

returning from somewhere else, anxiously asked when they would be reaching Borgo (LMj 10: 3).[4]

Bonaventure, to be sure that we do not miss the point, adds: "His mind was so fixed on heavenly splendors that he was not aware of the varieties of place, time, and people that he passed. That this happened to him often was confirmed by the repeated experiences of his companions" (ibid.). Thomas of Celano would surely agree with Bonaventure, for he writes: "Often as he walked along the road, thinking and singing of Jesus, he would forget his destination and start inviting all the elements to praise Jesus (1C 115).

Prior to this, Thomas of Celano paints a picture of a love-struck man: "The spring of radiant love that filled his heart within gushed forth. He was always with Jesus: Jesus in his heart, Jesus in his mouth, Jesus in his ears, Jesus in his eyes, Jesus in his hands, he bore Jesus always in his whole body" (1C 115).

The second quality of Franciscan prayer is, St. Bonaventure points out, the lingering desire to be alone with God:

> He had learned in prayer that the presence of the Holy Spirit for which he longed was granted more intimately to those who invoke him, the more the Holy Spirit found them withdrawn from the noise of the worldly affairs. Therefore seeking out solitary places, he used to go to deserted and abandoned churches to pray at night (LMj 10:3).

This desire is reminiscent of the lover who wants to spend time alone with the Beloved simply because the presence of the Beloved is a cause of delight and enjoyment. It is, then, not a disdain for the company of others. Rather it is an overwhelming desire to be with the one loved.

Bonaventure's third quality of a truly Franciscan appreciation of prayer is revealed in the midst of the temptations that Francis had during his lonely hours at night with the Lord. Bonaventure

---
[4] *FA:ED* 2, 606.

points out that the devil underestimated Francis's commitment to prayer. He had a "firmness of mind the devils could not bear"(LMj 10:3). This steadfastness to prayer on the part of the Poverello is a clear indication that the person who desires to become a prayer cannot confuse infatuation with love. Many are infatuated with the Lord. This lasts for a brief period of time until a new infatuation arises. Love, on the other hand, is unwavering in its craving for the divine presence.

Just as the body participates in lovemaking, it also participates in the life of prayer. This is clearly the tradition of the Song of Songs, which was a foundational spiritual document in the Middle Ages. Bonaventure presents Francis as a truly bodily person of prayer:

> When the man of God was left alone and at peace, he would fill the groves with sighs, sprinkle the ground with tears, strike his breast with his fist and having found there a kind of secret hiding place, he would converse with the Lord. There he would answer his Judge, there he would entreat his Father, there he would entertain his Friend (LMj 10:4).

Yet, when in public, Francis never wanted to make a show of his prayer life so "he used to expend the greatest effort to be like the others so that what he might show outwardly would not deprive him of his inner reward because of the glow of human attention" (LMj 10:4). Of course, this did not always work as is evident from the many dramatic accounts of Francis's life of prayer. Nor did the brothers think this appropriate, as is obvious from Brother Illuminato's advice to the Poverello:

> You must know that God sometimes shows you his divine mysteries not only for yourself but also for the sake of others. So it seems that you should rightly be afraid of being judged guilty of hiding your talent if you keep hidden something which God has shown you for the future good of many other people (Little Flowers, II, Third Consideration on the Holy Stigmata).

And Franciscan prayer affects others, as Bonaventure points out in recounting the story of the abbot from the monastery of St. Justin, who meets Francis along the road and asks him to pray for him, only to feel a warmth and sweetness within himself as Francis prayed for him (cf. LMj 10: 5).

To summarize, then, one becomes a prayer through a holy forgetfulness, a longing to be alone with the Beloved, a steadfast relationship with the Beloved, a love that is expressed through the body without being a show, and affecting others.

This approach to prayer so carefully described by Bonaventure was made by St. Clare into both an art and a way of life. For her, contemplation was in essence a love relationship that filled her with the light of her Beloved. She wrote to her friend Agnes of Prague "... totally love him who gave himself totally for your love, at whose beauty the sun and the moon marvel, whose rewards and their uniqueness and gradeur have no limits" (3LAg 15-16).[5] For Clare, contemplation is the embracing of the Beloved whose glory surpasses creation. This particular form of contemplation is often referred to as Bridal Mysticism. Clare's unique appreciation of this can be seen in her understanding of the enclosure, whose purpose was not to keep the world out but rather to be that intimate place where the heart becomes the dwelling place of the God she so loves. The enclosure, then, is sacramental: it is an outward sign of the heart's captivating relationship with the Beloved. So she enlightens Agnes by reminding her that "the faithful person... is greater than heaven itself, since the heavens and the rest of creation cannot contain their Creator, only the faithful soul is His dwelling place and throne" (3 LAg 21-22).

As mentioned above, beauty is an essential aspect of Franciscan prayer – thus it was for Clare. Likewise, Clare's contemplative consciousness can be described as a personal, loving relationship with Christ, like that of a bride whose Bridegroom intimately dwells within her. As any person in love, Clare and Francis probably experienced the temptation to

---

[5] *CA:ED*, 51.

remain exclusively with the One loved. Francis overcame such a temptation with the help of Clare and Brother Sylvester:

> These true proponents of justice conferred together about whether they should live among the people or go off to solitary places. Saint Francis did not put his trust in his own efforts, but with holy prayer coming before any decision, he chose not to live for himself alone, but for the one who died for all. For he knew that he was sent for this: to win for God souls which the devil was trying to snatch away (1C 35).

Francis and Clare, in their contemplative consciousness, knew they were called and sent for the sake of others so that even in their prayer lives, they could not exclude others. They knew that the gift given must be shared; love cannot survive in isolation. St. Bonaventure points this out magnificently when he writes of Francis's piety as a relational virtue founded on the relationships of the Trinity:

> True piety, which according to the Apostle is helpful for all things, had so filled Francis's heart and penetrated its depths that it seemed to have appropriated the man of God completely into its dominion. This is what drew him up to God through devotion, transformed him into Christ through compassion, attracted him to his neighbor through condescension, and symbolically showed a return to the state of original innocence through universal reconciliation with each and everything (LMj 8:1).

To have a contemplative consciousness, then, does not mean disassociating oneself from the world; rather it demands an involvement in the world, actively participating in the world to make it better. This prayerful stance is an integrating experience, uniting contemplation and action, justice and peace, and becoming ourselves by relating to others. Contemplative consciousness, understood by followers of Francis and Clare, is integral to the invitation to mission.

D. QUESTIONS

1. Look through Francis's writings, especially his prayers, litanies, and praises. What characteristics surface in them around his view of God, his method of prayer, and his understanding of prayer?

2. Explore how Clare's life in the cloister significantly colors her method of prayer and the images she uses to articulate her relationship with God.

3. What is the role of prayer in your life? How would you describe your method, your vision of God, and your understanding of the purpose of prayer.

4. How can prayer lead you to imitation of Christ?

5. How do you understand contemplation? Do you seek to contemplate God?

6. How does your contemplation lead to action, to love of your family, spouse, sisters and brothers? How does it relate to the hope of peace and justice in the world?

E. BIBLIOGRAPHY

Blastic, Michael. "Contemplation and Compassion: A Franciscan Ministerial Spirituality," *Franciscan Leadership in Ministry*, Spirit and Life, 7. Ed. Carrozo, Cushing and Himes, St. Bonaventure, NY: Franciscan Institute, 1991, 149-77.

Ingham, Mary Beth. *Rejoicing in the Works of the Lord: Beauty in the Franciscan Tradition*. Franciscan Heritage Series, 6. St. Bonaventure: Franciscan Institute, 2009.

Delio, Ilia. *The Humility of God: A Franciscan Perspective*. Cincinnati: St. Anthony Messenger Press, 2005.

Bartoli, Marco. *Saint Clare Beyond the Legend*. Trans Frances Teresa Downing. Cincinnati: St. Anthony Messenger Press, 2010.

F. Picture Credits

Vision of Saint Francis in the Fiery Chariot, Santa Croce Sacristy Panels, Life of Saint Francis

Unit Eight

Franciscan Presence & Dialogue:
Living with Diversity in a Pluralist Society

CONTENTS

From the Franciscan Sources

A.   Introduction

B.   Survey

C.   Information

D.   Questions

E.   Bibliography

F.   Picture Credits

From the Franciscan Sources

Francis used to gather up any piece of writing, whether divine or human, wherever he found it: on the road, in the house, on the floor. He would reverently pick it up and put it in a sacred or decent place because the name of the Lord, or something pertaining to it might be written there.

> Once a brother asked why he so carefully gathered bits of writing, even writings of pagans where the name of the Lord does not appear. He replied: "Son, I do this because they have the letters which make the glorious name of the Lord God. And the good that is found there does not belong to the pagans nor to any human beings, but to God alone 'to whom belongs all good things'" (1C 82).

A. Introduction

In our earlier units we learned that the Franciscan Movement is fundamentally missionary, meaning that we are sent with a Gospel message for our world. Every Franciscan-inspired person, then, participates in this evangelical dynamic, which has special features and basic attitudes, which can be summarized in the phrase Pax et Bonum, which literally means Peace and Good but by extension signifies Peace and Salvation, salvation being the greatest good that God offers to humankind. Peace will be dealt with in Unit 9. In this Unit we will deal with a Franciscan appreciation of salvation as the foundation for life in a pluralistic society.

B. Survey

Francis of Assisi, through his life and actions, gave a new initiative to the mission of the Church. Francis himself lived as a missionary among his fellow Christians as well as among the Saracens (medieval term for Muslims). He lived and preached the good news of Peace and Salvation, desiring that everyone embrace Christ and in doing so find salvation, that is, the good (bonum) that comes from living in the Kingdom of God. The person motivated by the mission-mindedness of Francis and Clare does not compel others to become Christians by threats of hell and damnation but shares his or her faith because of its meaningfulness in his or her life.

C. Information

Before the Second Vatican Council, salvation was generally understood as accepting the faith, receiving the sacraments and hoping for eternal life. However, the Franciscan perspective, which is far more in line with the thoughts of the Second Vatican Council, speaks of integral salvation, which is fundamentally fulfillment of our human needs spiritually, materially, socially, politically and progressively. God's invitation, then, is, in the words of the Franciscan expert on mission Arnulf Camps, "[a] dialogical invitation [which] stimulates us and incites us to work for the betterment of our total human condition so that the kingdom of God may come. . .a kingdom of love, justice, unity, and peace."[1] Such a sentiment reiterates the reflection of Pope Paul VI in a document entitled *Evangelii Nuntiandi*: we are called "to bring the Good News into all areas of humanity, and through its impact, to transform that humanity from within making it new."[2]

This perspective is grasped in the *Rule of the Secular Franciscan Order*, when it states:

---

[1] Arnulf Camp, "Franciscan Dialogue with Other Religions," *Build Up My Church: Franciscan Inspirations for and from the Third World*, ed. Leonardo Boff and Walbert Bulhmann (Chicago: OFM English-Speaking Conference, 1984), 135.

[2] Paul VI, *Evangelii nuntiandi* #18 (Washington: Publications Office, United States Catholic Conference, 1976).

Let [the Secular Franciscans] be active by the testimony of their own human life and even with courageous individual and communal initiatives, in the promotion of justice and in particular in the field of public life, committing themselves through concrete choices in harmony with their faith.[3]

With this outlook, we come to realize that salvation is a much broader term than it was at the time of Francis and Clare and that one of the repercussions of such a viewpoint is that one who is sent into the contemporary world is sent for very different reasons than in the days of Christendom. We are sent to share the Way that has been revealed to us for a better, more human existence in this world, which leads us into our future with God.

The Christian who understands this concept of salvation does not say "If you don't follow the Christian way, you'll go to hell" but "Let me share with you what has brought meaning into my life." A polemical attitude is replaced by a dialogical invitation. This approach is in imitation of the approach that God takes with us: he invites us into His life and Spirit so that we may have "Life and have it abundantly" (Jn 10:10). So dialogue is not a technique. It is a theological method based upon this understanding of God's invitation with the Lord. Hence the necessity of listening (cf. Units 5, 7).

Now the seemingly simple greeting of Francis, Pax et Bonum, is filled with new meaning, conveying Francis's response to the other as other, while it is also the warm greeting of a brother meeting a stranger only to discover a long lost and unknown brother or sister.

Before we can discuss the meaning of this dialogue along with its characteristics, it is important to know the basic attitudes we bring to that dialogue. These perspectives include:

• Affirming the Goodness of Life

---

[3] *SFO Rule,* http://www.nafra-sfo.org/sforule.html.

We live in pessimistic times. Perhaps this is particularly felt by those who lived through John F. Kennedy's Camelot and Pope John XXIII's aggiornomento. Neo-conservatives, fundamentalists, and restorationists overwhelm us. Drugs, murder, and domestic violence frighten us. Yet, beneath these ills of civil and ecclesial society, we maintain a Franciscan optimism toward life: it is good because it is a gift from God, misunderstood and misused at times, but a gift nevertheless. It has the potential for goodness and freshness among us. As the friars gathered at the 1971 missionary conference in Medellina observed:

> In spite of the darkness, we declare our faith and our undeniable hope.... This is no empty optimism, for our hope is Gospel-based and influenced by the tremendous good will of sincere and hard-working people the world over. Our guarantee is the certainty of the Gospel of Christ. Working together toward a genuine and realistic Franciscan response to the tensions and confusion around us, we turn to '"the Light of the World," Who alone gives us "living hope."[4]

• Relating as Brothers and Sisters

Again we turn to the friars gathered at Medellin, who stated that "our mission is not to lands but to people.... We desire to be their brothers [and sisters], their friends, their servants."[5] This has been emphasized repeatedly in past units.

• Respect for Cultures

When the Franciscan-motivated person encounters new cultures, especially those brought to our shores by new immigrants, he or she will "appreciate the cultural values of the

---

[4] "We are Sent: The Franciscan Missionary Vocation in the World Today," *Franciscan Missionary Charism in Contemporary Franciscan and Church Documents* (Quezon City: CCFMC Office, 1986), 116.

[5] "We are Sent ...," 118.

people and will sing the Canticle of Creation on seeing love, the sense of community, the dignity and the joy of the people: because it is all created by Him and through Him! With this theological interpretation, the Gospel will more easily be 'incarnated' within cultures and be made to take on local forms."[6] This will be further discussed in Unit 10.

• Respect for Religions

There is no clearer articulation of this than in Nostra Aetate, the declaration on the relationship of the Church to non-Christian religions, a brief but significant document from the Second Vatican Council, which states:

> The Catholic Church rejects nothing which is true and holy in these religions. She looks with sincere respect upon those ways of conduct and of life, those rules and teachings which, though differing in many particulars from what she holds and sets forth, nevertheless often reflect a ray of that Truth which enlightens everyone.... Prudently and lovingly, through dialogue and collaboration with the followers of other religions, and in witness of Christian faith and life, acknowledge, preserve, and promote the spiritual and moral goods among them, as well as the values in their society and culture.[7]

• The Common Search for Meaning

When we search for the meaning of life in general and our lives in particular, we can generally summarize the results of this search into three categories: beliefs, practices, and narratives. In other words, we find meaning in life when we are able to base our lives on truths bigger than ourselves, to articulate why we do what we do, and to share the stories that unite and motivate

---

[6] "Missionary Life and Activity," *Franciscan Missionary Charism in Contemporary Franciscan and Church Documents* (Quezon City: CCFMC Office, 1986), 185.

[7] *Nostra aetate, Vatican II Council II: The Conciliar and Post Conciliar Douments* (Collegeville: Liturgical Press,), 738.

us. All religions must grapple with these concerns and provide an encouraging response to the searches of believers.

For Franciscan-minded people, narrative holds a place of priority not only because the early Franciscan movement is primarily handed down to us through stories but also because stories inspire us. Often enough, while beliefs and practices may differ among world religions, there are extraordinary similarities in their narratives, not in the details but surely in their sweep.

In *Pursuit of a Vision*, the document on formation from Medellin, encourages the formators of the Order to teach new members to listen:

> The candidate should be carefully instructed in the art of dialogue and taught its nature, purpose, principles, conditions, methods, and forms. In the same spirit we must carefully avoid any words, judgments or actions which do not express the true condition of our separated brothers [and sisters]. We must take care to learn their history and mentality, give greater and clearer witness to our own faith, and encourage everyone to collaborate to the extent of his capability and the norms of the Church.[8]

This concise statement summarizes very well what is expected of any Franciscan-minded person who lives in a pluralistic society. Unlike Francis, Clare and their followers, we do not need to travel to far-off lands to discover people who think differently than we do, who have customs and practices which appear odd to us, and whose narratives are foreign to us. They live on our streets, shop in the same stores as we do, and have the same frustrations and concerns that we have. Sometimes they even pray in the pew next to us. Like us, they are men and women of good will, solid values, and generous spirit. To be argumentative and apologetic in a pluralistic society is simply to contribute to the "hot air" that already comes from our talk shows, adding to prejudice and hatred. To be good Christians today, then, we would be better served by studying *The Art of Dialogue* rather than *The Art of War*. The recent documents of

---

[8] "In Pursuit of a Vision," *The Medellin Documents* (New York: Communications Office of Holy Name Province, 1971), 38.

the Church emphasize this and the spirit of Francis and Clare requires it.

Even before studying some of the more significant documents, however, we must be convinced of the value of pluralism. Today pluralism is perceived a value in itself, while in previous times it was considered intolerable, at least officially, though it always existed in one form or another. Such a stance was justified by the principle of non-contradiction: logically, if there are diverse positions, ideologies and religions, they contradict one another. Therefore, one must decide which one is true and which false, which right and which wrong since all convictions cannot be equally true or right. Today, in our postmodern world, the conclusion of our syllogisms should begin not with "therefore" but with "nevertheless."

Without escaping into an untenable relativism, pluralism questions the "either/or" approach to life and its convictions. Pluralism recognizes the rich manifestation of an inexhaustible and boundless reality. So the differing views and perspectives of others are seen not as threats to our own firmly held beliefs but as ways of enlightening and challenging our own views and opinions. This new understanding encourages us to become acquainted with and to accept our pluriform world. Dialogue, then, has become a theological method which strives to restore and maintain peace and harmony in a highly pluralistic world.

During the Second Vatican Council, Pope Paul VI wrote the encyclical *Ecclesiam Suam*, which dealt with the ways in which the Church must carry out its mission in today's world. In this letter, Paul VI insisted on the priority of dialogue in the contemporary Church, basing his observations upon "the dialogue of salvation," that is, the conversation that God enters into with us. The Pope points out that this dialogue takes place through the spontaneous initiative of God, begun in charity, as an act of love to which one freely responds (cf. 72-75). The Pontiff provides four characteristics of Christian dialogue: clearness, meekness, trust, and prudence. He concludes that it is necessary to listen, not simply to the other's voice, but more importantly to his or her heart (cf. 80-81,87).[9]

---

[9] Paul VI, *Ecclesian suam* (1964). http://www.papalencyclicals.net/Paul06/p6eccles.htm, #72-75.

Since that time, many papal and congregational documents have been written about dialogue, perhaps the most important ones for our purposes being *Dialogue and Mission* (1984) and *Dialogue and Proclamation* (1991), both from the Vatican's Secretariat for Non-Christians. Both of these documents give us hints as how to live productively in a Christ-like manner in a pluralistic society. The former document distinguishes between four forms of dialogue: *the dialogue of life*; *the dialogue of action*; *the dialogue of theological exchange*; and *the dialogue of religious experience*. In a pluralistic society such as ours, it is quite common to be involved in the dialogues of life and action: we easily share our joys and sorrows, friendship and partnership with those with whom we live and work and we readily become involved in collaborative efforts to better the society in which we live. Professional theologians are involved in *the dialogue of theological exchange*. Perhaps most appealing to Franciscans is *the dialogue of religious experience*, which encompasses the sharing of one's life of faith and prayer, for, while Francis never proselytized, he never hesitated to profess his faith, especially in the primacy of Christ.[10] Such an existential approach is generally more easily accepted than a theoretical discussion. Such a conversation also will fulfill the aim of inter-religious dialogue, which, according to *Dialogue and Proclamation*, is to "deepen [one's] religious commitment, to respond with increasing sincerity to God's personal call and gracious self-giving which, as our faith tells us, always passes through the mediation of Jesus Christ and the work of the Spirit."[11]

"Sincere dialogue," then, "implies, on the one hand, mutual acceptance of differences, or even of contradictions, and on the other, respect for the free decision of persons taken according to the dictates of their conscience."[12] In that spirit, we can offer *A*

---

[10] "Paul VI, *Ecclesian suam* (1964). http://www.papalencyclicals.net/Paul06/p6eccles.htm, #80-81, 87.

[11] "Reflection and Orientations on Interreligious Dialogue and the Proclamation of the Gospel of Jesus Christ," *Pontifical Council for Interreligious Dialogue and Proclamation*, http://puffin.creighton.edu/jesuit/dialogue/documents/ articles/dialogue__and_proclamation.html.!984, #42.

[12] "Reflection and Orientations on Interreligious Dialogue and the Proclamation of the Gospel of Jesus Christ," *Pontifical Council for Interreligious*

Decalogue of Rules for Franciscan Dialogue which may help us to fulfill our mission in a pluralistic society:

- Franciscan Dialogue is animated by contemplative consciousness (cf. Unit 7);

- Enter the dialogue as a *minores*, avoiding quarrels and disputes while being subject to all (cf. ER 16);

- Be honest and upright, bearing witness that you are a Christian (cf. ER 16);

- Trust in the other, accepting his or her honesty and uprightness;

- Live among others with different faith and life views without fear or suspicion;

- Seize the initiative, as Pope Paul VI says "We must be the first to ask people for a conversation, not waiting for them to request an encounter with us";

- Share the Good News in word and deed, showing that this News is good more by what you do than by what you say;

- Work for the betterment of your world, especially those in need;

- Seek "to understand rather than be understood" especially in your ability to listen;

- And be an instrument of peace (cf. Unit 9).

The diversity with which we live in a pluralistic society, of course, is not merely religious. It is also a diversity of races, cultures, and political and moral perspectives, to use but a

---

Dialogue and Proclamation, http://puffin.creighton.edu/jesuit/dialogue/documents/ articles/dialogue-and-proclamation.htm. #40.

few quick examples. This Decalogue can be utilized in all circumstances and they can be summarized in one over-riding principle: God created this individual for whom I must have the utmost respect and reverence, which are virtues far beyond simple tolerance.

D. QUESTIONS

1. What is it like for me to interact with people who have different beliefs than I do?

2. How do I listen to others? How do I dialogue with others? I consider last time I had a serious (involving a difference of opinion) conversation with someone. What happened? Did I listen to her or his heart? Did I emphasize our differences or our common ground? What prevented me from being more open to the others' opinions?

3. How comfortable am I dialoguing with others from different traditions about issues of religious experience? How might I do this?

4. The prayer attributed to Francis of Assisi asks that we "seek to understand rather than to be understood." How do I express this in my ability/willingness to listen and be with others, especially those with different spiritual/religious perspectives?

5. What are my attitudes toward ecumenism, unity and oneness in the body of Christ?

6. What are my sources of information about those who are 'other'? What new sources of information might I look to in order to obtain a more balanced view?

E. BIBLIOGRAPHY

Fitzgerald, Michael and Borelli, John, ed. *Interfaith Dialogue: A Catholic View*. Maryknoll: Orbis, 2006.

Dardess, George. *Do We Worship the Same God?* Cincinnati: St. Anthony Messenger Press. 2006.

Dardess, George and Peggy Rosenthal. *Reclaiming Beauty for the Good of the World: Muslim and Christian Creativity as Moral Power*. Louisville: Fons Vitae, 2010.

Dupuis, Jacques. *Christianity and the Religions: From Confrontation to Dialogue*. Maryknoll: Obris. 2003.

A Common Word: Muslims and Christians on Loving God and Neighbor, Ed. Miroslav Volf, Ghazi bin Muhammad, Melissa Yarrington, Grand Rapids: Eerdmans, 2010.

F PICTURE CREDITS

St. Francis Preaching before Pope Honorius III, Upper Church, Assisi

Unit Nine

Franciscan Peace-Making in a Culture of Violence

CONTENTS

From the Franciscan Sources

A. Introduction

B. Survey

C. Information

D. Questions

E. Bibliography

F. Picture Credits

FROM THE FRANCISCAN SOURCES

St. Francis was staying in the town of Gubbio during the time when a fearsome wolf, rabid with hunger, was roaming the area, devouring people and animals. The people were so frightened that they carried weapons with them whenever leaving the city proper. But their weapons were inadequate against the starving wolf.

>The Saint, hearing about this, decided to go out and meet the wolf, even though the people of Gubbio warned him against this. However, Francis, arming himself only with the sign of the cross, went to meet the wolf, which came running toward him with its watering mouth wide opened.
>
>The Saint made the sign of the cross toward the wolf, crying out; "Brother Wolf, come to me. In the name of Christ, I order you not to hurt me or anyone else." At once the terrifying jaws of the wolf closed, he stopped running, lowered his head, and lay at the Saint's feet, as though he had become a lamb.
>
>The Poverello spoke to the wolf: "Brother Wolf, you are doing great harm here in Gubbio. You are committing terrible crimes for which you deserve to die. But I want to make peace between you and the townspeople." The wolf wagged his tail and shook his body in agreement.
>
>St. Francis then made a peace pact between the wolf and the people of Gubbio, the wolf agreeing neither to harm the people nor the animals of Gubbio and the people agreeing to feed the wolf, who was acting harmfully out of hunger.
>
>From that day, the people and the wolf kept the pact which Francis had made. The wolf lived two more years, during which time he went from door to door receiving

food from the people. He hurt no one and no one hurt him. And it is a striking fact that not even a single dog ever barked at him.

The wolf grew old and died. And the people were saddened because, whenever he went through town, his peaceful kindness and patience reminded them of the virtues and holiness of St. Francis (cf. Little Flowers 21).

A. INTRODUCTION

Perhaps no story about St. Francis is better known and less understood than the seemingly quaint account of the Wolf of Gubbio. Whether or not the wolf was real, the story is larger than the taming of the wolf. Its kernel deals with the ability of St. Francis to bring warring parties together through communication and compromise. As such, it provides us with Francis's approach to peace making: Francis relates as a brother, his only armor is the cross, he ascertains the cause of the savage behavior and finds an appropriate resolution to it, and so reconciles the warring parties.

B. SURVEY

St. Francis's commitment to peace is at the heart of his message. Having personally failed as a knight and a soldier, he came to realize the significance of peace to reconcile differences. Wherever peace is spoken of, his name is often mentioned. Even though falsely attributed to him, the famous *Peace Prayer* is an indication of how closely we link the *Poverello* with the desire to be an instrument of peace[1]. In this unit we will investigate how one becomes such an instrument according to the design of St. Francis of Assisi and his followers, particularly St. Bonaventure and St. Bernardine of Siena.

C. INFORMATION

---

[1] For more information on the *Peace Prayer* see Leonardo Boff, *The Prayer of Saint Francis: A Message of Peace for the World Today* (Maryknoll: Orbis, 2001).

Peace was at the heart of the Franciscan message from its inception. Francis and his brothers lived and preached peace, as is evident from Celano's words:

> Francis, Christ's bravest soldier, went around the cities and villages, proclaiming the kingdom of God, and preaching peace and penance for the remission of sins, not in persuasive words of human wisdom but in the learning and power of the Spirit (1C 36).

And St. Bonaventure adds that Francis greeted people with a message of "Peace:"

> In all his preaching, he announced peace by saying: "May the Lord give you peace." Thus he greeted the people at the beginning of his talk. As he later testified, he had learned this greeting by the Lord revealing it to him (LMj 3:2).

This greeting was not just a slogan. Rather, it was an authentic expression of the simple, non-violent way of life that Francis desired for himself and his followers. Francis forbade everything that thwarted peace and generated conflict among his brothers and sisters and in society at large. This is obvious from the *Rule* (LR 3:10): "I counsel, admonish and exhort my brothers in the Lord Jesus Christ not to quarrel or argue or judge others when they go about in the world; but let them be meek, peaceful, modest, gentle and humble, speaking courteously to everyone as is becoming." It is not insignificant that the very next line of that *Rule* forbids the brothers to ride horseback.

This radical position of St. Francis can best be understood when it is compared to the twelfth century work *In Praise of the New Knighthood*, written by St. Bernard of Clairvaux.

Francis certainly would have grimaced at Bernard's development of a "spirituality" for knights:

[The knight does not] bear the sword in vain, for he is God's minister, for the punishment of evildoers and for the praise of the good. If he kills an evildoer, he is not a mankiller, but, if I may put it so, a killer of evil. He is evidently the avenger of Christ towards evildoers and he is rightly considered a defender of Christians.... When he inflicts death, it is to Christ's profit.[2]

Such words are a far cry from the attitude of St. Francis, who preferred talking with the Sultan to killing him. In fact, Francis was so adamant in his desire that the friars not have arms that he connected this to his stance on poverty:

If we had any possessions, we would be forced to bear arms to protect them since possessions are a cause of dispute and strife, and in many ways hinder us from loving God and our neighbor. Therefore, in this life, we wish to have no temporal possessions (L3C 35).

Perhaps this admonition was the result of the intriguing story of the thief who became a friar. There was a small fraternity of friars who possessed little, but even that little was coveted by a local thief who regularly stole from the brothers. Frustrated, they decided to entrap him. But Francis personally put a stop to that. He urged them instead to invite the persistent thief to share the modest things they had. Reluctantly, the friars agreed. The highly unexpected result was that the thief joined the Order!

This prohibition to bear arms is quite explicit in the original *Rule* of the Secular Franciscans: "Deadly weapons may never be received for use against people nor may they be carried."[3]

The present *Rule* of the Third Order Regular Franciscans maintains that same spirit:

---

[2] Clairvaux, Chapter 3.
[3] *Memoriale Propositi*. VI:3. Cf. Robert Stewart, O.F.M., *De illis quifaciunt penitentiam: The Rule of The Secular Franciscan Order: Origins, Development, Interpretation* (Rome: Instituto Storico Dei Capuccini, 1991), 192. (Available from Franciscan Institute Publications, St. Bonaventure University.)

As they announce peace with their lips, let them be careful to have it even within their own hearts. No one should be aroused to wrath or insult on their account, rather all should be moved to peace, goodwill, and mercy because of their gentleness. The brothers and sisters are called to heal the wounded, to bind up those who are bruised, and to reclaim the erring. Wherever they are, they should recall that they have given themselves up completely and handed themselves totally to our Lord Jesus Christ. Therefore, they should be prepared to expose themselves to every enemy, visible and invisible, for love of the Lord because He says: "Blessed are they who suffer persecution for the sake of justice, theirs is the kingdom of heaven."[4]

The Franciscan stance for peace, then, was radical at its time and is still quite radical today, offering an alternative approach to conflict resolution through non-violence. Such an approach is evident in the story of the Wolf of Gubbio, which is a highly formalized account of the legal Renaissance document commonly called "an instrument of peace," for the reconciliation of warring parties: the savage is tamed by the words of a peacemaker, the aggressor swears an oath not to violate the legal agreement, and there is a public ritual, ordinarily ending with the kiss of peace between the parties in conflict. In short, "[this] passage is a metaphor of a flawless reconciliation."[5]

It is particularly significant to observe that Francis addressed the cause of the violent actions of the wolf: it was hungry. It is not enough to arrive at an easy and often temporary peace that does not change the structures of a society so that the actions will be repeated over and over again, not only by one party but by many of those in similar difficulties.

St. Bonaventure takes up this theme of peace as he begins his journey into God in the prologue of the *Itinerarium*:

---

[4] *Third Order Rule*, 20:30.

[5] Cynthia Polecritti, *Preaching Peace in Renaissance Italy: Bernardine of Siena and His Audience*, Dissertation for University of California at Berkley, 1988, 94. Also see Cynthia Polecritti, *Preaching Peace in Renaissance Italy: Bernardine of Siena and His Audience* (Washington, D.C.: Catholic Univeristy of America Press, 2000).

At the beginning of every sermon [Francis] announced peace; in every greeting he wished for peace; in every contemplation he sighed for ecstatic peace like a citizen of that Jerusalem of which the Man of Peace, who was peaceable with those who hated peace, says: "Pray for the peace of Jerusalem." For he knew that the throne of Solomon would not stand except in peace, since it is written: In peace is his place and his abode in Sion (Prol 1).

So Bonaventure tells us that he went to LaVerna, following the example of Francis, "... seeking this peace with painting spirit" (Prol 2). At this point in the history of the Order, Bonaventure and all the friars were in desperate need of peace, the Order was torn by conflict between the "Community" (brothers who wanted to live a relaxed form of their Rule) and the "Spirituals" (those who maintained that the Friars Minor were to continue living simply as stated in the Rule). As the newly-elected general minister, Bonaventure was expected to bring the conflict to a resolution, and he knew that he could not even attempt to bring about peace if he didn't have it within himself.

At LaVerna Bonaventure learned that, while he could not change these brothers, he could remain peaceful in the midst of conflict. It was his attitude that changed along with his desire to remain open and in conversation with even those friars who saw Franciscan life differently than did he.

Like Bonaventure, it is often difficult for the Franciscan-oriented person who sees the violence in society to grasp that peacemaking begins with oneself and one's attitude in dealing with that violence. Revenge is frequently the easier and quicker response to the violence we encounter. The death penalty rather than life in prison without the possibility of parole, prison rather than rehabilitation, hell rather than forgiveness seem almost to be spontaneous responses to society's ills. Such immediate reactions only indicate how far we are from the spirit of peacemaking advocated by St. Francis. Today revenge has a new and kinder name: closure.

While understanding and appreciating Bonaventure's emphasis on inner peace, later Franciscans never lost Francis's desire to be instruments of peace in civil society. The most successful example of this may well be the 15th century preacher, Bernardine of Siena. In fact, Bernardine is presented by his earliest biographer as the "preacher as peacemaker." The papers from his canonization process sum this up by stating that "he reduced enemies to peace and concord, ended scandals, quarrels, and disagreements, and everywhere sowed charity and extinguished ancient hatreds."[6]

In his own words, however, Bernardine knew that, when it came to peace-making, the inner reality had to be united to the external observation: "There are two peaces, the one within and the other without."[7] Perhaps he knew the medieval tale of the fox and the bird: a fox convinces a small bird that peace has been declared between birds and their predators. The skeptical bird hesitates to give the fox the required kiss of peace until the fox convinces him to do so because he freely closes his eyes. When the bird draws near, the fox devours him. Polecritti observes:

> [Bernardine's] special gift as a preacher was an ability to enter the minds of individuals and understand their hopes and fears in relation to others, his real goal a conversion which would then be reflected in an external sign, the ritual of peacemaking. But the interior peace was never easy to arrange in a culture where the fox still held sway.[8]

Franciscan peacemaking is no easy process as is obvious from the sad fact that that there is no evidence that such a peacemaking effort was ever even attempted between Francis and his father.

Perhaps no twentieth century person better exemplifies the Franciscan art of peacemaking through non-violence than Martin Luther King, Jr., who could well share with Bernardine the title of "preacher as peacemaker." Uniting the interior and

---

[6] Polecritti, *Preaching Peace...*, 126.
[7] Polecritti, *Preaching Peace...*, 124.
[8] Polecritti, *Preaching Peace...*, 126.

exterior, the personal and social dimensions of peacemaking, King was able to offer Jesus's command to love as more than a Utopian dream. It was for him the way to change the hatred and prejudice within the self and in society.

In a sermon entitled "Love Your Enemies," King offers three principles for peacemaking that are in accord with Francis's dealing with the wolf of Gubbio:

> First, we must develop and maintain the capacity to forgive.... Forgiveness does not mean ignoring what has been done or putting a false label on an evil act. It means, rather, that the evil act no longer remains as a barrier to the relationship;
>
> Second, we must recognize that the evil act of the enemy-neighbor, the thing that hurts, never quite expresses all that he is. An element of goodness may be found even in our worst enemy. This simply means that there is some good in the worst of us and some evil in the best of us. When we discover this we are less prone to hate our enemies. When we look beneath the surface, beneath the impulsive evil deed, we see within our enemy-neighbor a measure of goodness and know that the viciousness and evilness of his acts are not quite representative of all that he is;
>
> Third, we must not seek to defeat or humiliate the enemy but to win his friendship and understanding.... At this level we love men not because we like them, nor because their ways are appealing to us, nor even because they possess some type of divine spark; we love man because God loves him.[9]

King also offers three reasons for loving our enemies:

> First, returning hate for hate multiplies hate, adding deeper darkness to a night already devoid of stars. Darkness cannot drive out darkness; only light can do that. Hate multiplies hate, violence multiplies violence,

---

[9] Martin Luther King, Jr, *Love Your Enemies* (New York: Harper and Row Publishers, 1963), 35-40.

and toughness multiplies toughness in a descending spiral of destruction;

Second, hate scars the soul and distorts the personality. Mindful that hate is an evil and dangerous force, we too often think of what it does to the person hated, but hate is just as injurious to the person who hates. Like an unchecked cancer, hate corrodes the personality and eats away its vital unity;

Third, love is the one force capable of transforming an enemy into a friend. We never get rid of an enemy by meeting hate with hate; we get rid of an enemy by getting rid of enmity.[10]

All of this, whether from Francis or Bonaventure, Bernardine or King, may sound beautiful but also quite irrelevant. If so, then, one would have to admit that the Gospel itself is irrelevant or, as King says:

Of course, this is not practical. Life is a matter of getting even, of hitting back, of dog eat dog. Am I saying that Jesus commands us to love those who hurt and oppress us? Do I sound like most preachers —idealistic and impractical? Maybe in some distant Utopia, you say, that idea will work, but not in the hard, cold world in which we live.

My friends, we have followed the so-called practical way for too long a time now, and it has led inexorably to deeper confusion and chaos. Time is cluttered with the wreckage of communities which surrendered to hatred and violence. For the salvation of our nation and the salvation of mankind, we must follow another way.[11]

That way is the counter-cultural mission of those imbued with the Franciscan spirit: to tame the wolves of Gubbio, wherever they may be found.

D. QUESTIONS

---

[10] Martin Luther King, Jr, *Love Your Enemies*, 35-40.
[11] Martin Luther King, Jr, *Love Your Enemies*, 35-40.

1. What are the sources of violence in my community and country. What is my stance toward them? How do I bear witness to non-violence in a culture of violence? How does peace-making begin with me?

2. Do I believe that Jesus' commandment to "Love your enemies" has social/political implications? How do I live this out?

3. Who today embodies the spirit and commitment of non-violence of Jesus, Francis of Assisi, Gandhi, Dr. Martin Luther King Jr. in our world? In our Church?

4. Consider the relationships in your life. For which relationships are you grateful? Which relationships need to be improved or ended? What conflicts need to be named and resolved?

E. FURTHER READING

Boff, Leonardo. *The Prayer of Saint Francis: A Message of Peace for the World Today*. Maryknoll: Orbis. 2001.

Kraybill, Donald, Steven Nolt, David Weaver-Zercher. *Amish Grace: How Forgiveness Transcended Tragedy*. San Francisco: Jossy-Bass, 2007.

E PICTURE CREDITS

Catterdale di Pienza: Saint Francis and the Wolf

UNIT TEN

INCULTURATION AS A FRANCISCAN PERSPECITVE

Build With Living Stones 121

CONTENTS

From the Franciscan Sources

A.   Introduction

B.   Survey

C.   Information

D.   Questions

E.   Bibliography

F.   Picture Credits

From the Franciscan Sources

When Blessed Francis was at Saint Mary of the Portiuncula for the general chapter known as the Chapter of Mats because the only dwellings there were made of rush-mats, there were five thousand brothers present. Many wise and learned brothers went to the Lord of Ostia, who was there and told him: "Lord, we want you to persuade Brother Francis to follow the advice of the wise brothers and allow himself to be guided by them." They cited the Rule of blessed Benedict, blessed Augustine, and blessed Bernard which lay down the principles of a regular life.

> The cardinal related everything to blessed Francis, giving him some advice as well. The blessed Francis took him by the hand, saying nothing, and led him to the brothers assembled in chapter, and spoke to the brothers in the fervor and power of the Holy Spirit: "My brothers! My brothers! God has called me by the way of simplicity and humility, and has truly shown me this way for those who want to trust and imitate me. Therefore I do not want you to mention to me any Rule, whether of Saint Augustine, or of Saint Bernard, or of Saint Benedict, or any other way or form of life except the one that the Lord in his mercy has shown and given to me. And the Lord told me what He wanted: He wanted me to be a new fool in this world. God did not wish to lead us by any way other than this knowledge, but God will confound you by your knowledge and wisdom. But I trust in the Lord's police that through them God will punish you, and you will return to your former status, with your blame, like it or not."
>
> The cardinal was greatly shocked, and said nothing, and all the brothers were greatly afraid (2MP 68).

A. Introduction

The sense of exasperation that Francis exhibited toward those brothers who were flirting with the danger of compromising his intuition to live the Gospel in a new way could readily be explained by his stubbornness or by his fear of studies or even by a certain selfishness on his part to have his own way and name it the Lord's. However, none of these reasons sufficiently grasp the evangelical insight of the *Poverello*: he wanted to live the Gospel in his own culture without assimilating the negative traits of that culture. Francis wanted what neither Bernard, Benedict, nor Augustine could accomplish with their emphasis on a stable lifestyle. He wanted to be among the people: "he wished the brothers to live in leper-houses to serve them..." (2MP 44). Francis knew the difference between inculturation and assimilation.

B. Survey

For Francis and his followers, the *Rule* developed from the lived experiences of the friars rather than as predetermined regulations for every situation. The Franciscan *Rule*, then, admits of adaptation to the cultural situations in which the friars are. As such, it provides us with hints of a recently developed notion: inculturation.

This Unit will deal with inculturation from a Franciscan perspective, defining it, describing its process, and applying it to our call to mission.

C. Information

In his classic text *Christianity Rediscovered*, Vincent Donovan, C.S.Sp., tells the story of his amazing experience of nearly twenty years in East Africa among the Masai people. It is a lengthy, first person account of the essential role which inculturation plays in preaching the Gospel. Donovan writes of his missionary work in Kenya and Tanzania, where the Masai live as nomads; however, his experience is easily translated to

Inculturation Through a Franciscan Perspective

every part of the world where serious efforts are being put forth to make the Good News of Jesus understandable and accessible to different cultures.

Donovan begins with a statement of futility and frustration: after many years in Masailand, he and the Holy Spirit missioners who preceded him there had nothing to show for their evangelizing efforts. In fact the missionaries had come to the conclusion that the Masai were impermeable to the Gospel and impossible to convert. This, of course, produced something of a crisis among the Western priests of the community. If one people could not accept the universal message of Jesus, then what can one say about that message?

Christianity Rediscovered is the story of "one more try." It tells of a final attempt at approaching the Masai, taking seriously this people's culture and not allowing for any overlay of Western Christianity to obscure what the missioners called the "naked Gospel" – the life and teaching of Jesus in its barest essentials. They understood that as "an evangelist, a missionary must respect the culture of a people, not destroy it"… (pg. 24) When Donovan and a few others went back to the Masai villages asking if they might sit down with the communities and discuss Jesus' way of life, the elders asked: "why has it taken you so long to come to this point with us? You came to build schools and clinics, with medicines and pencils in order to entice us into accepting your religion; now we will hear you as equals."

The results of this "experiment" with the Masai were spectacular in terms of conversion and especially in terms of their unique appropriation of Catholic Christianity. For example, because of the community-oriented Masai culture, the rite of initiation which we call Baptism and in our Western minds understand as an individual matter, became totally communal for these indigenous Africans. Whole villages would go to the river for this ritual, and those in the community who understood it committed themselves to assisting those who didn't. The entire village would accept this "Way" because they were a village – a community which said "*WE* believe."

When the community received baptism, the missionaries asked them "What will you call yourselves?" Since there is no Masai notion or word for church, the Masai reflected on the question and finally answered, "When we are baptized we will become ... the age group brotherhood of God." In *Christianity Rediscovered* Donovan explains that "brotherhood" (*orporor*) is the most sacred notion in their culture, the most important value in their tribe, and they had chosen it as the word for Church.

These are examples of what has come to be known as "inculturation," which can most easily be described as the interaction between the Gospel and culture. Or in the words of the Jesuit sociologist John A. Coleman: "Inculturation is the existential dialogue between a living people and the living Gospel."[1] Bonaventure, Giotto, Dante, and many others of their times understood that the Gospel had to be transmitted into the culture so that it could be discovered through the culture.

Pope Paul VI grasped this:

> Christian life should not only be adapted to the forms of thought and custom which the temporal environment offers and imposes on her, provided they are compatible with the basic exigencies of her religious and moral program, but it should also try to draw close to them, to purify them, to ennoble them, to vivify and sanctify them.[2]

The Pontiff repeats this sentiment time and again, especially in his ground-breaking *Evangelli nuntiandi*, suggesting that there is a natural variety of expressions of our one faith:

> What matters is to evangelize humankind's culture and cultures (not in a purely decorative way, as it were, by applying a thin veneer, but in a vital way, in depth and right to their very roots) ... taking the person as one's starting-point and always coming back to the relationships of people among themselves and with God ... the Kingdom which the Gospel proclaims is lived by men and women who are profoundly linked to a culture, and the building

---

[1] Coleman, "How Culture and the Gospel Meet and Interact," *Origins*, 6/7/01. Vol 31:4, 64.

[2] Paul VI, *Ecclesiam suam*, "Paths of the Church," par. #42, August 6, 1964. www.catholic-forum.com/saints/pope0262d.htm.

up of the Kingdom cannot avoid borrowing the elements of human culture or cultures.³

These sentiments echo the words of Saint Augustine:

> What we have in common is the annual celebration of the Passion, Resurrection, Ascension of the Lord, the Coming of the Holy Spirit, or whatever the whole Church observes where it exists. Other customs differ according to region, country and village. Some fast on the Sabbath, others do not. Some receive the Body and Blood of Christ daily, others only on certain days. In some places the Eucharist is celebrated daily, in others only on the Sabbath and Sunday, in still others only on Sunday. These and similar practices are a matter of free choice. A sensible and genuine Christian does not rate one practice better than another, but rather follows the practice of where he or she actually is.⁴

Saint Francis, in the *Rule* of 1223, understood this when he mandates that the ministers be concerned about the needs of the friars "according to places, seasons, and cold climates" (LR 4).

A directive in 1659 from the Congregation for the Proclamation of the Faith, the highest mission authority in the Church at the time stated in a letter to the Apostolic Vicars in China:

> Put no value in and persuade the people under no pretext to change their rites, habits and customs, unless they are clearly against the religion and good morals. For what would be more absurd than to bring France, Spain, Italy or another part of Europe to China? Do not bring these things there.
>
> Bring the faith, which does not scorn or damage the rites or healthy customs of any people but on the contrary

---

³ Paul VI. *Evangelii nuntiandi* (Washington: Publications Office, United States Catholic Conference, 1976), par. #20.

⁴ St. Augustine, *On the Customs of the Church*, #42.

wants to see it strengthened and protecte. Try to follow their customs as closely as possible.⁵

The Second Vatican Council rediscovered this experience of inculturation when it re-emphasized the importance of the local church. The bishops gathered at the Council stated in the Dogmatic Constitution on the Church: "While safeguarding the unity of the faith and the unique divine constitution of the universal church, local churches enjoy their own discipline, their own liturgical usage and their own theological and spiritual heritage" (LG 23).

We would be naive to think that because it was said at the Council, it has been accomplished. In fact, at the gathering of Cardinals in Rome in May, 2001, the Franciscan Cardinal Aloisio Lorscheider told the Pope and his peers: "The decisions of Vatican Council II are not being applied, and we all suffer, at the local level, from a distant bureaucracy that is increasingly deaf."⁶ Perhaps the relationship between the universal and local churches is the most bitterly contested issue in the Church today. To put it simply, it revolves around a key concern: is the Church to be transplanted or planted, or discovered and cultivated?

Oftentimes in the history of the missiology, the Church has opted for and implemented the transplantation of the Roman Church into native lands. This is evangelization without taking into account the culture of the people receiving the Good News. European theology, Roman regulations, liturgical practice and ecclesial customs are simply transplanted from Rome to the native land. Prior to Vatican II, this was even presented as an ideal: no matter where the Catholic traveled in the world, Mass was experienced by the traveler exactly the same way as it was at home. This transplantation was in fact the sociological experience of assimilation: Rome assimilated the new culture into its own culture.

The history of mission to the Americas is filled with stories of transplantation, especially in "New Spain," in which the friars were involved, traveling with the colonizers to bring Spain to

---

⁵ *Instructio Vicariorum*, Congregation for the Proclamation of the Faith, 1659, #702.

⁶ Aloisio Cardinal Lorscheider (*New York Times*, 5/22/01).

America. For these conquerors, the Church was just one aspect of colonization. To preach the Kingdom was to preach the superiority of one's own culture.

Fortunately, there were exceptions. The efforts of the Franciscan Bernardo of Sahagun (1500-1590) made a very serious effort not to transplant the Roman Church but to plant the Word of God into the native culture, thus establishing the universal Church in and through a particular culture. He founded a college to train lay Indians to oversee ecclesial concerns and to prepare Indians for the priesthood. This effort for an indigenous culture was astonishing for the times. After ten years, Bernardo's efforts failed due to the opposition from the Spanish Crown, the hierarchy and even Bernardo's own friar-brothers. This experience, had it been allowed to grow, would have been an excellent example of inculturation: bringing the universality of the Church into a culture which would have been the setting for a living Church. Such a mission process demands that the one sent knows both the realities of the Church as well as the new culture in which he or she is living so that the Church is expressed theologically, liturgically, artistically, and practically within the atmosphere in which people live their daily lives. The Gospel then takes root in the culture, making Joseph's robe more brilliant and colorful.

Inculturation differs from assimilation. In assimilation, the Church would simply become part and particle of the culture. However, there are aspects of every culture that need to be "baptized" so that the sinful aspects of a culture may be either transformed or eliminated. Franciscans today speak of the need to be "counter-cultural," meaning that they must stand against those aspects of their cultures that are against their Gospel commitment and its values. When taking this stand, we must be cognizant of John Coleman's warning: "In being counter-cultural, the Catholic strategy must rely on and relate to already existent strands of restraint and correction within the culture and not crudely import foreign models or appeal to some untypically Catholic view of the Gospel as simply timeless and beyond culture."[7] There are many significant points in this caveat.

---

[7] Coleman, "How Culture and the Gospel Meet," 64.

American Catholics have too readily "imported" their faith rather than engage in the tiring and time-consuming process of inculturation. Whether the import is from Rome or Lima, it still does not excuse American Franciscans from theologizing and working within their own cultures which are many and diverse. Further, the timelessness of the Gospel message cannot be used as an excuse to create a disincarnate faith; we are a people of the Incarnation. The message must also be timely.

Inculturation requires a great deal of prudent discernment to determine those aspects of a culture that must be rejected and those that should be embraced. One must possess a living faith molded by one's culture along with an appreciation for the character, lived situation, and experiences of the native culture where the Gospel is being planted.

Recent understandings about inculturation as reviewed in this unit are in synch with the new style of religious life Francis gave birth to in the early 13th century. As friars were sent out to new locations Francis insisted upon utter respect for each person and cultural situation the brothers encountered – from the leper colonies to the cities and communes "beyond the Alps" to the Muslim camps. As they traveled to share the Gospel message with people who had not heard it, their preaching ushered in an innovative approach. Essential to the proclamation of the Word of God were behaviors of courtesy and respect, of listening and invitation, of openness and discovery, of building relationships. Their method of approaching the other and sharing the Good News was rooted in Francis's vision of universal kinship of all people. (Recall units 5 and 8.) In the redemptive love of God incarnated in the birth, life, death and resurrection of Jesus – Francis's vision required a different way of being among "non-believers" and sharing the Gospel message. It was the way of discovering the presence of God already alive in each place, among the people. It included discovering with and through the people, the truth of God's mystery and bounty, God's humility and majesty. Indeed, a new kind of fool was afoot in the world, and the Gospel was experiencing a re-birth! Such is the power of Franciscan inculturation.

D. Questions

Once in a lecture Vincent Donovan spoke of a Vatican visitation made to East Africa by some unnamed curial bureaucrat for the purpose of investigating the methodology, content and outcome of this evangelization among the Masai people. In his report to Rome the man described, critically, what was going on in Masailand as "the Gospel out of control."

Without knowing it, this Western, church-bound cleric had put his finger on what inculturation does in proclaiming the life and message of Jesus the Christ. The Gospel does "spin out of control" in such scenarios.

For us then the question becomes: what would the Gospel sound like, how would it be lived if our American culture were given the kind of attention which Vincent Donovan and his colleagues gave to the Masai traditions? Would not the Gospel of the one about whom it was said "it is better for one man to die than for the nation to perish" (John 11:50) – would not that Gospel challenge, shake, undermine and ultimately topple what Pope John Paul II called the "culture of death" in the industrialized West? Would not this American Empire and its subservient churches be locked in a life and death struggle if Christians here took the Gospel seriously?

There are graced dimensions in Western culture. Our individual freedoms, due processes and inviolable human rights, to name just a few, point to a highly developed respect for each citizen in most of our countries. However, the shadow side of our culture – individualism, hedonism, consumerism, militarism, etc. are antithetical to the life and message of Jesus. True inculturated evangelizing would severely challenge and ultimately undermine much of what we accept as normal in our societies.

Evangelical inculturation is a dangerous business. It has produced countless martyrs since it crashed onto the world stage in the first century CE. In our times evangelical inculturation has give the world Oscar Romeros, Dorothy Stangs, Dorothy Days, Martin Luther Kings, Dietrich Bonhoeffers, to name just a few.

The question faces us, then: shall we take seriously our culture and measure it against the life and teaching of Jesus? Or shall we continue to homogenize, trivialize and neuter this Gospel which we have received from the Son of the one who prayed to God "who has scattered the proud in the conceit of their hearts; who has cast down the mighty from their thrones and raised up the lowly; who has filled the hungry with good things and sent the rich away empty"? (Luke 1:51-53)

Other questions to consider:

1. The 2010/11 film, "Of Gods and Men," represents the thrust of missionary activity as more PRESENCE than direct evangelization (in the traditional sense of preaching, etc.). Do you feel that this is a valid form of evangelization even in a Western society?

2. How have you experienced being evangelized by another? How did you react?

3. Do you enjoy speaking to others about your faith? When have you spoken to others about your faith? How does it feel to be questioned about your faith? If you are uncomfortable speaking about your faith, what might change that for you?

4. Why was Francis's method of sharing the faith with others so unique? What are some of the attitudes and or values underlie such an approach to sharing one's faith?

5. What are some movies that by exposing different perspectives (religious, cultural, gender, racial, etc.) , have opened new horizons for me

E. BIBLIOGRAPHY

Donovan, Vincent. *Christianity Rediscovered*. Maryknoll: ORBIS Books (25th Anniversary Edition), 2003.

Fox, Thomas. *Pentecost in Asia: A New Way of Being Church*. Maryknoll: ORBIS Books, 2002.

Irarrazaval, Diego. *Inculturation: New Dawn of the Church in Latin America*. Translated by Philip Berryman. Maryknoll: ORBIS Books, 2002.

Monti, Dominic. *Francis and His Brothers: A Popular History of the Franciscan Friars.*" Cincinnati: St. Anthony Messenger Press, 2000. Particularly pp 105-154.

Faith and Culture Series. *Contextualizing Gospel and Church*. Maryknoll: ORBIS Books, 2000.

F. PICTURE CREDITS

St. Francis Giving His Mantle to a Poor Knight, Upper Church, Assisi

Unit Eleven

A Franciscan Perspective on the Economy and the Global Reality

CONTENTS

From the Franciscan Sources

A. Introduction

B. Survey

C. Information

D. Questions

E. Bibliography

F. Picture Credits

From the Franciscan Sources

Francis's father hurried to the palace of the commune complaining to the city magistrates about his son and asking them to make him return the money he had taken from the house. When the magistrates saw how distraught he was, they sent a messenger to summon Francis to appear before them. Francis told the messenger that he had been freed by God's grace and, since he was a servant of almighty God alone, was no longer bound to the magistrates. The magistrates, unwilling to force the issue, told his father: "Because he is in the service of God, he no longer falls within our power."

Realizing that he could accomplish nothing with the magistrates, he made the same complaint before the bishop of the city. The bishop, a discerning and understanding man, duly called Francis to appear in order to respond to his father's complaint. Francis answered the messenger: "I will appear before the Lord bishop, because he is the father and lord of souls."

Then he came before the bishop and was received by him with great joy. The bishop said to him: "Your father is infuriated and extremely scandalized. If you wish to serve God, return the money you have to him, because God does not want you to spend money unjustly acquired on the work of the church. Your father's anger will abate when he gets the money back. My son, have confidence in the Lord and act courageously. Do not be afraid, for He will be your help and will abundantly provide for you with whatever is necessary for the work of the church" (L3C 6:19).

A. Introduction

In the time of Francis of Assisi, a word to indicate success would have been: "Cloth." In his doctoral dissertation *Bonaventure, John Paul II and a Humane Economy*, Daniel Pattee puts it this way: "Cloth was a status symbol; one person could readily size up another just by the clothes they were wearing. Francis had not only aspired to wearing nice clothing and becoming a cloth merchant like his father, he also learned to make use of money and the skills needed to procure it. He was, in the words of Celano, a shrewd businessman.[1] Of course, Francis grew to hate money and to wear patched clothes. These were not simply acts of piety; they were also social statements.

B. Survey

Frequently during the history of Franciscan-inspired life, Francis's conversion account has been reduced to a story of the playboy turned penitent, emphasizing Francis's individual conversion and avoiding the context in which that conversion took place. Francis's conversion was a response to the social context in which he lived: he wanted to make the Gospel a vibrant reality in his changing economic times. His lifestyle, especially his strong reaction to money, had and still has economic implications, which will be investigated in this Unit.

C. Information

When Francis of Assisi heard Christ's command to rebuild His house, he responded like a typical businessman. To accomplish such a task, he needed tools and mortar; he needed money to acquire these things. Armed with cloth to sell, he rode off to Foligno, where he proved himself an extraordinary businessman by not only selling the cloth but also the horse. Returning on foot to Assisi, he was ready to begin his commissioned work. His gravely disappointed father, however,

---

[1] Daniel Joseph Pattee, *Bonaventure, John Paul II and A Humane Economy* (Ann Arbor: UMI Dissertation Services, 2000).

had other ideas. In his disappointment and perhaps even more in his embarrassment, Francis's father sought to have him exiled from the area: Let him act mad in another part of Italy, but not in Pietro Bernardone's backyard. Francis's father should not be reduced to the mean stepmother of the Cinderella story. After all, he showered his son with the best, yet his son seemed prone to continual failure, first as a knight and soldier and later as a businessman and merchant. And Pietro Bernardone was well within his rights, as is obvious from the statutes of the commune of Assisi: "The son who does not give obedience to his father and to his mother, at their request is to be banished from the city and from the district, and no one may give him anything to eat or drink or help him in any way." Of course, Francis escaped such banishment by appealing to his newfound identity as a servant of God.

Francis's act of disrobing was as much a social and political action as it was a spiritual one. In Bonaventure's presentation, this is a threefold act: standing naked in the square, being covered with the bishop's mantle, and putting on the garment of the penitent. So this socio-political action had three implications: first, a renunciation of the present economic situation, the acceptance of the Church's blessing on this evangelical project, and the embrace of a new way of life that was contrary to the social values of Assisi. As a famous saying goes: "Francis stood *against* Assisi long before he became Francis of Assisi." The *Testament* of St. Francis clearly indicates that his conversion implied a change in social status. He says that he "left the world," that is the emerging world of profit economics. To appreciate this, we must understand the economic reality of Assisi at the time of Francis's conversion.

Lester Little, in his masterful *Religious Poverty and the Profit Economy in Medieval Europe*, distinguishes between the *gift economy* that preceded the Middle Ages and the *profit economy* that developed during the Middle Ages. In a gift economy, he says, "Goods and services are exchanged without having specific, calculated values assigned to them. Prestige, honour, and wealth are all expressed in the spontaneous giving of gifts," while "In a market economy, where one expects everything to have an assigned value, haggling, politeness, and fair-mindedness do sometimes have their place."[2] Francis, Clare and their followers lived during the transition from a gift economy to a profit economy. This raised as many spiritual questions for them as economic ones, especially as the friars moved into the cities. In a profit economy, urban dwellers who had money made it work for them, thus gaining more money. Franciscan preachers such as Bernardine of Siena and John Capistran preached strongly against this new economy by condemning usury. Their well-known anti-Semitism may well have stemmed more from usury than from ethnicity, since most moneylenders at the time were Jewish.

Bernardine is recognized as the founder of pawnshops where the poor could get needed funds without losing their goods permanently. After all, the friars knew the difficulties of the poor as city dwellers. One late thirteenth century friar, Bonvicinus of Ripa in his work *The Marvels of the City of Milan*, writes: "After what has been said [about the advantages of life in Milan], it is evident that in our city, life is wonderful for those who have enough money."[3]

The spirituality of Francis and Clare can fundamentally be identified as *gift spirituality* rather than *profit spirituality*. Since all good gifts come liberally from God, they must be shared with others; things are for our use rather than our possession; and, most significantly, voluntary poverty becomes a real value within this spirituality because economics has a role in our journey into God.

In a little known though well thought out work *De Superfluo*, St. Bonaventure addresses the economic realities of necessities and superfluities. There are in life, Bonaventure proposes, certain necessities without which we cannot survive. It is a simple fact that we need some material goods for human survival. These requirements are not unlike Maslow's *hierarchy of needs*. In Bonaventure's view, everything else is superfluous, that is, while it may enhance human existence, it is not required for it.

---

[2] Lester Little, *Religious Poverty and the Profit Economy in Medieval Europe* (Ithaca: Cornell University Press, 1987), 4.

[3] Bonivincus of Ripa, *The Marvels of the City of Milan*.

In typical fashion, Bonaventure makes further distinctions, indicating that some superfluous goods may be useful and necessary (a) for oneself, (b) for others, or (c) neither for oneself nor for others.

In the first case where some superfluous goods may be useful and necessary for oneself, for example, I may need more than another because of my physical condition or my social status. If I suffer from a disease that requires medical care and medicine, I have a right to what may be superfluous to others. A contemporary example may be the right that the elderly should have to prescription drugs, a right that the young do not have from age alone. In a similar fashion, my status in life may give me the right to what may be superfluous to others. For example a highly educated person may develop greater needs which would include such seemingly superfluous things as books, theatergoing, and entrance to museums.

In the second instance where some superfluous goods may be useful and necessary for another, Bonaventure posits the right of another to have more than he or she needs in order to serve others better. Such a person possesses more material goods than others in order to share them with those who cannot fulfill their own basic needs. For example, a rich person may be able to justify his wealth by the charities that he or she supports that aid the hungry, the sick, or the incapable.

In the final situation superfluous goods may not be accrued for oneself nor for another if such an accumulation neither serves one's own well-being nor the well-being of others. For example, I own exquisitely priced paintings in an exclusive penthouse, while the poor are starving in the streets far below.

From Bonaventure's presentation, a basic principle of Franciscan poverty emerges: one cannot possess superfluous goods to the detriment of those who do not even have the necessities of life.[4]

---

[4] St. Bonaventure, *De Superfluo* (See Ermenegildo Lio, O.F.M., *San Bonaventura e la questione autografa De superfluo; contenuta nel MS. di Assisi*, Bibl. Comun. 186 citata al Concilio Vat. II. Testo con studio critico-letterario e dottrinale (Rome: Facultas Theologica Pontificiae Universitatis Lateranensis. 1966).

This guideline is surely based upon the *Rule* of 1223 in which Francis admonishes his friars:

> Wherever the brothers may be and meet one another, let them show that they are members of the same family. Let each one confidently make known his need to the other, for if a mother loves and cares for her son according to the flesh, how much more diligently must someone love and care his brother according to the Spirit.[5]

The fundamental concept here is the sharing of God's good gifts, a theme taken up by the Second Vatican Council, when, in the "Pastoral Constitution on the Church in the Modern World," it observed:

> Every person has the right to possess a sufficient amount of the earth's goods for oneself and one's family. This has been the opinion of the Fathers and Doctors of the Church, who taught that people are bound to come to the aid of the poor and to do so not merely out of their superfluous goods.[6]

The Council Fathers, then, broaden the focus by insisting upon the Christian's need to share not only from his or her superfluities but also from life's necessities.

Mose Durst, in an article on what he calls "Principled Economics," says: "Religious people are not fools, and economists are not scoundrels. Yet, they each become foolish scoundrels if they ignore the understanding of the other in seeking to solve [the problems of poverty and injustice]."[7]

However, followers of the Franciscan Way would not set themselves up as judges of the rich, becoming cranky critics of their way of life. Francis warned his brothers "never to judge or

---

[5] Rule of 1223, 6: 7-8, *Francis of Assisi: Early Documents* (New York: New City Press, 1999), 1, 103.

[6] *Gaudium et Spes, Pastoral Constituion on the Church in the Modern World,* #69, *Vatican Council II, The Conciliar and Post Conciliar Documents,* ed. by Austin Flannery, O.P. (Collegeville: Liturgical Press, 1979).

[7] Mose Durst, "Essays Toward a Principled Economics," http: // www.tparents.ord / Library / Unification/ Books/Econ7Econ-05.htm.

criticize those who live in luxury, eat fastidiously, and indulge in superfluous and splendid clothes..."(L3C 58; cf. *Rule* of 1223: 2, 7). After all, while the economy divides us into rich and poor, the Gospel calls us to be brothers and sisters.

Franciscans deal with the economy as a significant aspect of their mission because it often is a major source of dehumanization in our society for the rich as well as the poor. Leonardo Boff, the Brazilian theologian, puts it this way:

> Poverty dehumanizes rich and poor alike. In the first place, the poor: poverty carries with it all kinds of needs; it destroys emotional life, one's relationship with others; it continually places obstacles in the way of the essential vocation of human beings to develop themselves and expand their abilities beyond the survival instinct; it leads them to envy, hatred, violence against those responsible for their misery, and often, against God, raising their fist against heaven.
>
> It dehumanizes the rich because it leads them to consider the poor as inferior, outcasts of society, the dead weight of history.... [They have] a profound scorn for the poor. They consider them to be socially disqualified; they avoid contact with them, going around them, insensitive to their misery.[8]

If this is the case, then, the poor need to be destereotyped. As Durst observes: "What the poor need, if they are to be lifted out of poverty, is first to be understood in a holistic way: as creative human beings in the context of family and community." Later, he further comments: "The removal of poverty is not an emergency action, but an ongoing process. A Principled Economics approach to poverty first focuses on the nature of the poor: individuals created in the image of God who have infinite potential, creativity, and value."[9] Franciscans who voluntarily accept poverty are called to witness to the nature of the poor and to speak for the involuntarily poor. Their concern is not primarily structures.

---

[8] Leonardo Boff, *Francis of Assisi: A Model for Human Liberation* (Maryknoll: Orbis, 2006), 45-46.

[9] Mose Durst, note 7 above.

Rather it is the persons who act within the structures. To change the people, of course, is ultimately to change the structures in which people operate.

To accomplish this, Franciscans in recent years have made a *preferential option for the poor*. This concept, from liberation theology, fundamentally means that Franciscans opt to see reality, and particularly economic reality, from the perspective of the poor. As Leonardo Boff comments: "What makes the poor poorer is the fact of generally being considered from the point of view of the rich. The greatness of St. Francis consisted in seeing the poor with the eyes of the poor, allowing him, thusly, to discover the values of the poor." This is certainly clear from the early Sources. Celano writes:

> The holy lover of complete humility went to the lepers and lived with them, serving them most diligently for God's sake and wash-ing all foulness from them, he wiped away all corruption of the ulcers (ICel 17).

And:

> The Father of the poor, the poor Francis, conforming himself to the poor in all things, was grieved when he saw someone poorer than himself, not because he longed for vainglory, but only from a feeling of compassion. And, though he was content with a tunic that was quite poor and rough, he frequently longed to divide it with some poor person (ICel 76).

In other words, after his conversion, Francis understood that he must share out of life's necessities, not out of his superfluities, as he had before his conversion. This suggests a new way of viewing our entire life in Christ including our mission.

In a working paper prepared for a Provincial Chapter, the friars of Holy Name Province observed:

> By option is meant a clear and continuing choice to be in solidarity with a certain segment of society —the poor.

This choice goes beyond the selection of future ministries and includes an intellectual, emotional, spiritual and physical taking sides with the poor. Opting for the poor means looking at life through their eyes, seeing reality from their vantage point, interpreting the "signs of the times" as they would. Such a conversion in perspective does not seem possible without direct contact with the poor. We have to be able to put names and faces on what otherwise becomes an abstract reality...No longer would personal or even institutional considerations be decisive in judging government, ecclesial, or congregational policies. Rather, their impact on the poor would become decisive.

The compassionate minister seeks to be "a voice for the voiceless" by calling attention to those whom others neglect. But such a minister does not attend to the outcast from outside of his condition, but as much as possible from within their place in society. This is eminently in line with the Franciscan tradition of poverty. In our work with the middle class, professionals, wealthy or powerful people, our standing in solidarity with the poor brings to them the faces of poverty. In our embrace of Poverty, we testify that it does exist in our societies, and that it is unacceptable. To do this, we have to be aware of the poverties in our world, be moved by the Lord's compassion over them, and thereby take on the 'mind of Christ' by opting for the poor.[10]

This is an extraordinary challenge, for it truly demands a conversion, a turning around to view all of reality, but especially the economy, from the vantage point of the poor. This will help us to develop a spirituality that is truly evangelical and Franciscan rather than pious and otherworldly.

D. Questions

---

[10] Provincial Chapter, Holy Name Province, 1983.

1. What is it like for me to be treated unfairly? What difference can an advocate make?

2. What are some of the justice issues in my local community? Are there any organizations addressing these issues? What kind of help are they seeking?

3. Where does concern for the injustices of this world fit into my thoughts and life?

4. How does the wisdom of Francis speak to our global concerns and economic issues? In what ways does that wisdom challenge me? What changes might it be suggesting for me?

E. BIBLIOGRAPHY

Boff, Leonardo. *Francis of Assisi: A Model for Human Liberation*. Maryknoll: Orbis, 2006. Particularly 43-92.

Cusato, Michael F. "Alms-Asking and Alms-Giving as Social Commentary and Spiritual Remedy," *The Rule of the Friars Minor, 1209-2009: Historical Perspectives, Lived Realities*, Spirit and Life 14 (St. Bonaventure, NY: FIP, 2010), pp. 59-79;

Cusato, Michael F. "The Early Franciscans and the Use of Money," *Poverty and Prosperity: Franciscans and the Use of Money*, Washington Theological Union Symposium Papers (2009), CFIT/ESC-OFM Series 9 (St. Bonaventure, NY: FIP, 2009), pp. 13-37.

Flood, David. *The Daily Labor of the Early Franciscans* (St. Bonaventure, NY: FIP, 2010).

Flood, David. *Work for Everyone: Francis of Assisi and the Ethic of Service*. Quezon City: CCFMC, 1997.

Todeschini, Giacomo. *Franciscan Wealth: From Voluntary Poverty to Market Economy* (St. Bonaventure, NY: FIP, 2009).

F. Picture Credits

Mystic Marriage of Saint Francis (Marriage of Saint Francis to Poverty), 1437

UNIT TWELVE

GENDER: REALITIES, STUMBLING BLOCKS
AND BREAKTHROUGHS

CONTENTS

From the Franciscan Sources

A.   Introduction

B.   Survey

C.   Information

D.   Questions

E.   Bibliography

F.   Picture Credits

FROM THE FRANCISCAN SOURCES

The footnote for the text below is worthy of consideration before reading the excerpt. It reads:

This narrative of 2C 112, unlike many other narrative in Book Two, is not found in any earlier source. Notice the contrast between the harshness of this number with the earlier story in 2C 38, also found in AC 69, that highlights Francis' warmth upon "seeing" the "very refined and delicate" noble lady from Volusiano. For other examples of Francis's response to women, see 2C 53, 59, 60, 86, 92, 95, 132, 155, 157. It seems that in 2C 112 issues of the 1240's are attributed to Francis. Although echoing monastic encouragement of caution and respect regarding relationships with women, this negative attitude is not evident in his writings or in other earlier texts. For one who in his writings never even mentions Eve in his accounts of the Fall, the above narrative of 2C 112 is not consistent. (*FA:ED* 2, 321)

He ordered avoiding completely honeyed poison, that is, familiarities with women, by which *even* holy men *are led astray*. He feared that in this the weak spirit would quickly be broken, and the strong *spirit often be weakened*. He said that avoiding contagion when conversing with them, except for *the most well-tested*, was as easy as *walking on live coals without burning his soles*, as Scripture has it. But in order to speak by action, *he showed himself an exemplar of virtue.*

Indeed the female even troubled him so much that you would believe this was neither caution nor good example, but fear or terror. When their inappropriate chattering made for competition in speaking, *with face lowered* with

Build With Living Stones

a humble and *brief word*, he called for silence. Sometimes, with his eyes *looking up to heaven*, he seemed to draw from there what he replied to those who *were muttering from the ground*. Women in whose minds the urging of holy devotion had made a home for Wisdom, he taught in wonderful but brief conversations.

When he spoke with a woman, he would speak out in a loud voice so that all could hear. He once said to his companion: "I'll tell you the truth, dear brother, I would not recognize any woman if I looked at her face, except for two. I know the face of this one and that one, but any other, I do not know."

Well done, father! For looking on them makes no one holy. Well done, I say, for that brings no gain, but rather, much loss, at least of time. They are an obstacle to those who want to undertake the hard journey, and look on the *face full of grace*.

A. Introduction

Francis had a peculiar relationship with women. On the one hand, he was a product of his age, in which every woman was an Eve, ready to tempt Adam, the man. Therefore she is to be avoided. On the other hand, in additon to his mother, Pica, the sources reveal the names of three women with whom Francis developed significant relationships. First there was Clare, the foundress of the Poor Clares, whom he called *la Cristiana* because for him she was the quintessential Christian woman. Then there was the woman of Volusiano, who was abused by her husband and who came to Francis for advice and direction; Francis helped her and her husband to participate in the evangelical life of penance according to their life situation. And there was Jacoba of Settesole, a noblewoman, whom he visited when he was in Rome, and whom he called "brother." Her presence and gifts consoled him on his deathbed. His relationship to women was, therefore, not without contradiction. It seems that it was not until the end of his life that he managed to achieve an inner freedom, when in his illness he allowed himself to become close to Clare and her sisters (cf. 3C 37).

B. Survey

Gender discriminiation presents a great challenge to the Franciscan family, which must continually examine itself as to how much it is affected by sexist ideas and mechanisms. This is the only way our family can offer a witness of genuine brotherhood/ sisterhood.

For Franciscan-minded men and women the following of Jesus implies that we are sisters and brothers to every person. We are called to familiarize ourselves with the reality and the life circumstances that mark the faith and self-image of those with whom we live and whom we serve, but that is not enough. We are called to feel the fears and sorrows, as well as the humiliation and suffering of our brothers and sisters just as Francis united himself with those who were marginalized by the society of Assisi. Indeed, we are called to uphold and witness to the dignity of each person and all peole. As brothers and sisters in a single family, we can bear witness to the possibility that women and men can share life creatively with one another. However, even in the Franciscan family there are some particulars that we should think about in the light of the knowledge that we have gained from a more in-depth study of the Franciscan sources.

C. Information

Over the centuries, the Franciscan narrative has mainly been researched, translated and studied by men. The viewpoint of these educated Franciscans was presumed to be valid for all the members of the Franciscan family, male and female. The feminine viewpoint was not represented in these interpretations of the narrative. Today we have come to appreciate the fact that the feminine voice widens the horizons of thought and provides insight into our common Franciscan story.

In recent years a growing number of women from the second and third orders had joined in the scientific study and pastoral applications of the Franciscan sources, providing a more balanced view of the Franciscan sources.

In our opening story, we took one example from the many found in the Franciscan sources, in which "woman" is identified with evil or sin. Such a negative attitude towards women is based, among others things, on the Genesis account of the Fall, resulting in men's fears of being tempted or of becoming influenced by a woman. When we read this selection, a number of different reactions may have surfaced in us:

• Accepting the negative image of women found in the Franciscan sources;

• Allowing the misleading image of women in the Franciscan sources to stand as is;

• Holding that the distorted image of women found in the sources is basically false; or

• Interpreting the Sources to discover new and meaningful elements hidden in them.

The last reaction provides the best hope for retrieving the fullness of the Franciscan narrative, for it reconstructs the tradition within its historical setting according to a theological method that respects and mirrors modern-day concerns and issues. This is the approach we will use in this Unit.

In analyzing Francis's relationship to women, his attitude toward power, privilege and prestige is significant.

According to the American psychologist Carol Gilligan, each person must decide for himself or herself whether to be guided primarily by a sense of justice or a sense of compassion. She claims that, in agreement with cultural conditioning, a sense of justice predominates among men, while among women it is a sense of compassion. The ethic of justice is identified with rights, rules and competition; in contrast, the ethic of compassion is identified with relationships, responsibility and cooperation.[1] From our reflections on the Franciscan heritage, we now know that it is primarily a tradition of compassion, perceiving rights and rules to be at the service of its compassionate mission.

Francis's convictions about minority and the servant style of his leadership bear the stamp of the Johannine understanding of "discipleship" (Jn. 13:1-20), providing a new approach to power, authority and obedience. The role and function of a minister is fundamentally different from the role of a prior or an abbott (ER IV; LR VII). Thus, an alternate approach arose to the hierarchical structure in the other religious orders of Francis's day.

Francis and Clare sought to promote and maintain a discipleship of equals in accord with the example of Jesus. In their Rules, they emphasized an ethic of compassion, which serves as the basis of their ethic of justice.

Both Francis and Clare had the ability to see life from a maternal perspective uniting responsibility and caring with justice. They emphasized the relationships of the brothers and sisters with one another. Institutions and structures were admittedly important to them, but relationships were even more important.

Fraternity, as Francis understood it, did not rely on a brother's good or failed behavior. For Francis, efforts to build genuine relationships were more essential and necessary in community life than the desire to act correctly out of a sense of justice or duty.

Today when we speak of minority, we include women in the circle of the poor, the excluded and marginal groups. In this way, solidarity with women and "living among them" (ER IX:2; XVI:3) becomes a central question: What does it mean for the Franciscan family if women—not of their free choice but because of oppressive structures —must play the role of *minores* in the Church and society?

With this in mind, we will now look at a variety of Franciscan accounts from a feminist perspective in order to discover new insight from these accounts.

---

[1] Carol Gilligan, *In A Different Voice: Psychological Theory and Women's Development* (Cambridge: Harvard Press, 1982).

Feminist thought critiques patriarchalism. This provides a perspective on the account of Francis's persecution by his father. Pietro Bernardone tries to force his own will and plans on Francis by humiliation, subordination and physical violence. However, Francis refused to be dominated, personally, politically or financially, and consequently rejected the power, privilege and nmstige of his father.

Lady Pica, Francis's mother, understood this father-son conflict. In solidarity with her son, she went against her husband—fully conscious of the personal risk this decision entailed. She freed her son from his father's chains, and so she was also maltreated, because her husband regarded her as a collaborator with an incorrigible son.

When Pietro Bernardone saw his power in the household being challenged and undermined, he sought legal redress. Since Francis was under the Church's jurisdiction, Pietro Bernadone turned to Bishop Guido, himself a patriarchally privileged man. Francis's father falsely presumed that Guido would, in the name of God, ensure the father's authority, honor and demands.

However, Guido sided with Francis, knowing quite well that such a stance went against tradition, something stood up which the Church herself usually. Of course, Guido could have refused to get involved in this squabble. After meeting Francis, however, he really had no choice.

Like Francis, Lady Pica and Bishop Guido, we too are faced with decisions involving traditional injustices, and this harkens back to patriarchal structures with which we must grapple.

In the story of the unnamed noblewoman of Volusiano, who was horribly mistreated by her husband (2C 38), our attention is drawn primarily to the conversion of her husband. Reading this from a woman's viewpoint, however, what really stands out is Francis's dialogue with this victim of domestic violence. The wife was in conflict with her husband. Thanks to Francis of Assisi, however, the husband comes to realize that his wife has the right to live her vocation and exercise self-determination. Eventually they both joined the penitential movement.

The story of "Brother Jacoba" has a special place in Franciscan tradition. It furnishes us with an example of Francis countermanding a rule that he himself wrote. Ordinarily Francis did not allow women to enter the Portiuncula enclosure of the friars, but the doors were opened for Jacoba; the regulation no longer applied. Incidentally, this shows Francis's attitude toward regulations. His call to "Open the doors and bring her in. The decree about women is not to be observed for Brother Jacoba" (3C 37) still holds true today. In the Franciscan family, women must not be excluded merely because they are women.

In recent years, our understanding of Clare has grown. In her writings she proves to be a determined woman as well as a spiritual director. Francis not only lifted the regulation against entrance into the Portiuncula for Clare and her Sisters but also sought her advice.

Throughout her life Clare resisted the Church's authority by her insistence on poverty. She was obviously more than Francis's "little plant!" For Pope Gregory IX, too, Clare was a spiritual authority, such that when he visited San Damiano he asked her to bless the bread at the table (LFl 33).

Clare's spiritual leadership is shown in her correspondence with Agnes of Prague. As a woman, she vicariously accompanied Agnes on her spiritual journey and supported her in her struggle with the Pope for spiritual autonomy:

> What you hold, may you always hold,
> What you do, may you always do and never abandon.
> But with swift pace, light step, unswerving feet,
> So that even your steps stir up no dust,
> May you go forward
> Securely, joyfully, and swiftly,
> On the path of prudent happiness,
> Not believing anything,
> Not agreeing with anything
> That would dissuade you from this resolution
> Or that would place a stumbling block for you on the way,
> So that you may offer your vows to the Most High
> In the pursuit of that perfection
> To which the spirit of the Lord has called you (3LAg: 11-14).

Clare's outspoken feminine consciousness is also clear in her Rule. For the very first time in history, a woman wrote a rule for women. In the formulation of her "Blessing," she emphasizes the feminine form of speech, which was unusual for traditional Church language.

In the name of the Father and of the Son and of the Holy Spirit.
  May the Lord bless you and keep you.
  May He show His face to you and have mercy on you.
  May He turn His countenance to you and give peace

to you, my sisters and daughters, and to all others who come and remain in your company and to others both now and in the future, who have persevered in every other monastery of the Poor Ladies.

I, Clare, a servant of Christ, a little plant of our most holy Father Francis, a sister and mother of you and the other poor sisters, although unworthy, beg our Lord Jesus Christ through His mercy and the intercession of His most holy Mother Mary and blessed Michael the Archangel and of all the holy angels of God, of our blessed Father Francis, and all men and women saints, that the heavenly Father give you and confirm for you this most holy blessing in *heaven* and on *earth*: on earth, by multiplying you in grace and His virtues among His servants and handmaids in his Church Militant; in heaven, by exalting you and glorifying you among His holy men and women in His Church Triumphant.

I bless you during my life and after my death, as I am able, out of all the blessings, with which *the Father of mercies* has blessed and will bless His sons and daughters *in heaven* and on earth and a spiritual father and mother have blessed and will bless their spiritual sons and daughters. Amen .

Always be lovers of your souls and those of all your sisters. And may you always be eager to observe what you have promised the Lord.

May the Lord always be with you and may you always be with Him. Amen. (BlCl)

A work, written in the middle of the thirteenth century, the *Sacrum Commercium or The Sacred Exchange between Saint Francis and Lady Poverty* has previously been limited to an understanding of the virtue of poverty. When we read it from a feminine perspective, however, totally new aspects surface.

Lady Poverty's attitudes and actions were similar to God's behavior toward God's chosen people. Likewise, the brothers' experience with Lady Poverty parallels the relationship between God and the prophets of Israel.

The literary genre which presents the "marriage" of Francis and Lady Poverty is the bridal mysticism of the Wisdom literature, some of the prophetic books and the *Song of Songs*. The lover and the beloved become one flesh and one spirit. Lady Poverty is the beloved bride, with whom Francis, the *alter Christus*, has entered into an indissoluble bond. Lady Poverty is the feminine likeness of the Crucified:

> You, most faithful spouse, most sweet lover, did not abandon him for a moment. Moreover, the more you saw him despised by every-one, the more you clung to him. For if you were not with him, he could never have been so despised by all (ScEx:20)!
>
> You did not abandon him even to death, death on a cross. And on that cross, his body stripped, his arms outstretched, his hands and feet pierced, you suffered with him, so that nothing would appear more glorious in him than you (ScEx:21).

Medieval women identified with the Crucified. Often that led to passivity and to silence about injustice and oppression, even to the acceptance of their own oppression as women. Lady Poverty, in contrast, presents the liberating image of redemptive suffering that is born out of solidarity. Fearlessly and passionately she enters into the mystery of the cross. With her whole being she accepts the incarnate God; as a "woman" she embraces God, and embodies the divine suffering in her own. Through her radical and sincere union with the crucified, Lady Poverty invites the brothers to leave behind all smugness and self-satisfaction. She challenges her sisters to go beyond pity and doubt:

> Let the length of the race and the immensity of the labor not deter you for you will have a great reward. While focusing on the author and goal of all good, the Lord Jesus Christ, who, after he condemned its shame, endured the cross (Heb. 12:2) for the sake of the joy that awaited him, hold onto the unwavering confession of your hope (Heb. 10:23). Run in love to the race that is set before you (Heb. 12:1). Run with the patience which is especially necessary for you, that, while you are doing God's will, you may receive what is promised (Heb.10:36) (ScEx 66).

Gender discrimination (sexism) is a social sin. By recognizing the prejudices, errors and blind spots that have affected our vision and hindered us in the following of Christ, Franciscan-minded people can counter this social sin with the wisdom of our tradition. It is as widespread as racism, class consciousness and militarism. Our own particular, Franciscan-shaped witness to a community of divine love, the Trinity, demands that liberating attitudes and action bring about the full participation and the human dignity of all our sisters and brothers.

Because of our conviction "that only in mutual giving and receiving will we be able to realize our Franciscan vocation,"[2] we accept the challenge to confront and eliminate sexism in all its visible and hidden forms.

D. QUESTIONS

---

[2] "The Inter-Franciscan Document, Mattli, 1982," *Franciscan Missionary Charism in Contemporary Franciscan and Church Documents* (Quezon City, Philippines: CCFMC Office, 1986), 227.

1. What have women's voices offered the Church? How have they shaped the Christian tradition? How has the Church heard them? Who are speaking for women in the Church today and in what kind of work have they inserted themselves?

2. Identify important voices in the history of feminism. What have women gained from this hard fought journey? What work is still left to do?

3. How have I embraced both the feminine and masculine dimensions of my identity? How do I express the two poles of my soul in my prayer? in my ministry? in my relationships?

4. How do gender roles still play a role in the work place, in the home, in the Church? Are there truths to the roles? What roles do you carry and do you feel yourself oppressed by them?

5. What aspects of Franciscan spirituality foster an inclusive attitude?

E. BIBLIOGRAPHY

Fiorenza, Elizabeth Schussler. I*n Memory of Her: A Feminist Theological Reconstruction of Christian Origins*. New York: Crossroads, 1984.

La Cugna, Catherine (ed.). *Freeing Theology: the Essentials of Theology from a Feminist Perspective*. San Francisco: Harper, 1993.

Nothwehr, Dawn. *The Franciscan View of the Human Person: Some Central Elements*. St. Bonaventure: Franciscan Institute, 2005.

Pryds, Darleen. *Women of the Street: Early Franciscan Women and their Mendicant Vocation*. St. Bonaventure: Franciscan Institute, 2010.

Schneiders, Sandra M. *With Oil in Their Lamps: Faith, Feminism, and the Future*. Mahwah, NJ: Paulist Press, 2000.

F Picture Credits

The Bishop of Assisi Handking a Palm to Saint Clare

UNIT THIRTEEN

BROTHER SUN AND SISTER MOON:
A FRANCISCAN VIEW OF CREATION

CONTENTS

From the Franciscan Sources

A. Introduction

B. Survey

C. Information

D. Questions

E. Bibliography

F. Picture Credits

FROM THE FRANCISCAN SOURCES

How great do you think was the delight the beauty of flowers brought to his soul whenever he saw their lovely form and noticed their sweet fragrance? He would immediately turn his gaze to the beauty of that flower, brilliant in the springtime, sprouting from the root of Jesse. By its fragrance it raised up countless thousands of the dead. Whenever he found an abundance of flowers, he used to preach to them and invite them to praise the Lord, just as if they were endowed with reason. Fields and vineyards, rocks and woods, and all the beauties of the field, flowing springs and blooming gardens, earth and fire, air and wind: all these he urged to the love of God and to willing service. Finally, he used to call all creatures by the name of "brother" and "sister" and in a wonderful way, unknown to others, he could discern the secrets of the heart of creatures like someone who already passed into the freedom of the glory of the children of God (1C81).

A. INTRODUCTION

We live in an age of ecological deterioration which is unfortunately caused by our environmentally dangerous high-tech lifestyles, and often justified by the Genesis account of creation, which presents creation as at humankind's disposal. Yet we cannot survive without the ecosystem we are destroying. We cannot live without plants and trees, animals and vegetables. The attitude of St. Francis may seem to be merely romantic and sentimental, perhaps even slightly mad. On the other hand, perhaps Francis's view can challenge us to reverse this ecological crisis by providing an alternative view to the utilitarian model in the contemporary reading of the creation accounts, which seem to be understood by some as an endorsement for our unlimited exploitation of creation.

B. Survey

The nature stories recounted about Francis are poetic and often very beautiful. They are so numerous that, even if some of them are pious inventions, they undoubtedly establish a central message: all of creation with its rich diversity reveals the Triune God. There are ramifications to this message, namely that the Franciscan mindset and lifestyle acknowledge all of creation as partners and companions in life, offering a remedy for our lack of concern over the precarious state of earth and its creatures as a religious issue. Surely, God's creation is useful to humankind. However, we do not stand apart from creation; rather, we are a part of it. We are God's creation along with wolves and lambs, stones and flowers, sky and stars. Together we form God's body.[1]

C. Information

In November, 1979, Pope John Paul II named St. Francis of Assisi the patron saint of ecology, commenting: "St. Francis is justifiably ranked among those famous saints who have respected nature as a marvelous gift of God to humankind. He knew how to honor each one of the works of the Creator. Moved by the divine Spirit, he also sang the magnificent Canticle of the Sun, in which he first and foremost gave praise, glory, honor and thanksgiving to the Supreme, Almighty and Good God for Brother Sun, Sister Moon and the stars of heaven."[2] This was no empty gesture on the part of the Holy Father, for Francis encountered God's creation with respect and tenderness:

---

[1] Sallie McFague, *Super, Natural Christian: How Should We Love Nature?* (Minneapolis: Fortress Press, 1997), 57.

[2] *Inter Sanctos*, "Peace with All Creation." *Bulletin Institute for Theological Encounter with Science and Technology*, Winter, 1990. vol. 21, No. 1, 10.

• Whenever Francis washed his hands, he chose a place where his feet did not step on "Sister Water, who is very useful and humble and precious and chaste." (CtC 7);

• He walked on rocks only lightly, out of his love for Jesus who was his rock (2C 165);

• Whenever the brothers went out to cut trees, Francis instructed them to take care of the trees, cutting down only one part, leaving a bit of the stump behind so that the tree might regenerate (2C 165);

• He advised gardeners not to transform all their acreage into arable land, but to leave an area for meadows where herbs and flowers could grow wildly (2C 165. Clare expressed a similar provision in her Testament. See TestCl 53-55.);

• He treated lights, torches and candles with care so as not to dim their brightness which represented the eternal Light (2C 165);

• He lifted worms from the street so that they would not be trampled upon (1C 80);

• He gave bees honey and sweet wine so that they would not die in winter (2C 165);

• He bought sheep about to be slaughtered in order to free them (1C 77);

• He treated the lamb, the symbol of Jesus, with particular fondness (1C 77);

• And, of course, he wrote the *Canticle of the Creatures*.

Perhaps no one expressed this Franciscan appreciation for God's world more perceptively than the theologian Romano Guardini when he wrote in *The Living God*:

> Have you ever noticed how a child treats things? The things around it seem to come alive. When a child takes things into its heart and hands they acquire a strange freedom. They mean much more than they do to us adults. They have quite a different depth. Something behind them is released. They confide in one another. A form that is normally hidden appears, and this is the real thing. Things speak; they are on intimate terms with one another and with the child; they become friendly and attractive and strong and dangerous in quite a different way. But then the child grows older and becomes rational, it wants to use things, to control and enjoy them, and then they shrivel up. Occasionally the mystery emerges again, in the spring perhaps, when everything is stirring with new life, or in the hovering darkness of the night.
>
> There are adults who seem to have similar influence on the things around them but on a higher plane. St. Francis was one such person. The reports of how he called the fishes and preached to them, how he spoke to the birds of the glory of God, how the wolf of Gubbio heard and obeyed his warnings, are no doubt legendary but it is significant that such legends should have been woven around a man at all. It means that this Francis of Assisi was one in whose presence things were different from what they are in the presence of ordinary human beings. In his presence they acquired a new nature. They were released from their dumbness, their fetters fell away from them, stunted things blossomed and became beautiful, free, and noble. More than that, something entirely new was awakened in them. This was not a fairy story, but a miracle. Not in the usual sense but in the sense that in the presence of this true child of God and his conspicuously blessed "glory" something from God entered into them— and this was what they had been waiting for, longingly and painfully,

something in which their innermost spirit was fulfilled and in which they were enabled to be wholly themselves for the first time. This was what people felt, and to express what they felt they produced these legends about St. Francis. What St. Paul had in mind began to be true: "or the creature was made subject to vanity, not willingly, but by reason of Him who hath subjected the same in hope. Because the creature itself shall be delivered from the bondage of corruption into the glorious liberty of the children of God." This glorious liberty of the children of God began to be revealed in St. Francis and around him. In his presence the world began to be redeemed. In his eyes and his heart and hands things began to be different. This is a mystery full of great promise.[3]

Yet the Franciscan eco-feminist Gabriele Uhlein asks: "Can the great Franciscan *Canticle* speak to those who no longer have access to naturally pure water, fresh air, or uncontaminated food?" Surely "[W]e cannot sing the *Canticle* as Francis did." Her point is well taken. In an age of oil spills, toxic emissions, greenhouse gas, and a fragile ozone layer Francis's words may appear a bit naive. However, Uhlein encourages us "[to] respond to Francis's example of *Canticle*-making.'"[4]

Fundamental to this *Canticle*-making is a view of nature from more than the utilitarian interpretation of the Genesis creation accounts that see nature's worth solely in its service to humankind. It was Francis's genius to perceive the intrinsic worth of nature. In her small volume entitled *A Franciscan View of Creation: Learning to Live in a Sacramental World*, Ilia Delio notes:

> Francis came to understand that all creation, like himself, is called to give praise and glory to God. He lived in love, and, by loving other creatures, let them be, encouraging

---

[3] Romano Guardini, *The Living God*, trans. Stanley Godman (New York: Pantheon Books, 1957), 106-08.

[4] Gabriele Uhlein, "Creation: A Franciscan Conversion Conversation," in *In Solitude and Dialogue*, ed. A. Carrozzo (St. Bonaventure, NY: The Franciscan Institute, 2000), 53.

them to grow in their uniqueness, sharing with them their very being. Everything spoke to Francis of the infinite love of God. Trees, worms, flowers by the side of the road – all were for him saints gazing up into the face of God. Creation became the place to find God and, in finding God, Francis realized his intimate relationship to all of creation.[5]

Each and everything that exists is of value in itself but also as a symbol or sacrament of its Creator, and as a revelation of Christ, after Whom it is patterned. To fully grasp this, one must appreciate Francis's understanding of the sacrament of the Eucharist.

Writing to all the friars, Francis says:

kissing your feet with all that love of which I am capable, I implore you to show all possible reverence and honor to the most holy Body and Blood of our Lord Jesus Christ in Whom that which is in heaven and on earth has been brought to peace and reconciled to almighty God (LtOrd 12).

These seemingly simple words reveal a profound message: Francis, at the feet of his brothers as Jesus was at the feet of his disciples during the Last Supper, appreciates the Eucharist far beyond the transformed bread and wine. These humble gifts of creation impact all of creation. As the Jesuit natural scientist and philosopher Teilhard de Chardin declared, these elements of the earth have a cosmic dimension: bread and wine become the living presence of the Lord so that the world may become His body. In Chardin's words, the cosmos is in the process of "Christification."

The three authors of *Care for Creation: a Franciscan spirituality of the Earth* address the profound relationship between our response to the Incarnation, the Word made flesh and to the biological community of Earth. They raise questions such as

---

[5] Ilia Delio, *A Franciscan View of Creation: Learning to Live in a Sacramental World* (St. Bonaventure: Franciscan Institute Publications, 2003), 12.

- How should we relate to creation?

- How can we understand the human journey to God as one that includes creation?

- How can the tradition help us overcome violence to creation and restore relationships of peace and justice?

- Is it enough simply to "recycle" or "turn off the lights" or does our tradition call us to a more radical stance with regard to creation?[6]

The authors raise a series of valuable considerations, three of which we include here:

1. We must realize our interconnectedness to creation. Part of our poverty is to realize our dependency on the things of the created world.... A new consciousness must call us to an active stance as "brother" and "sister" to the nonhuman creation.

2. Following the Franciscan emphasis on a Christ-centered universe, contact with nature needs to be a fundamental component of our Franciscan way of life. A trip to the ocean, a walk in the woods, working in the garden are important not primarily for what they produce, but for their inherent Christ-contact.

3. We must realize that our sinful actions are at the root of our present ecological crisis and thus our need for ongoing penance or conversion. The Franciscan practice of penance embodies humility. It consists in acknowledging our brokenness and sinfulness. The practice of "Eco-penance" is both an interior attitude and a praxis. It can

---

[6] Ilia Delio, Keith Warner, Pamela Wood, *Care for Creation: a Franciscan spirituality of the Earth* (Cincinnati: St. Anthony Messenger Press, 2008), 204.

promote consistency between the statement of values we make about creation and our behavior toward it.[7]

In 1992, this attitude was eloquently expressed in a Declaration of the Franciscans in the United Nations:

> An ecological perspective allows us to develop a new spirituality anchored in the Franciscan charism. All creatures are related to each other in universal fraternity. Humanity recognizes itself as a part of a cosmic unity encompassing the whole creation. Only the human person can consciously welcome other creatures who are different and live among them responsibly, neither destroying nor dominating them. We acknowledge the earth as our mother for it produces and preserves life; we call her sister because, together with her, we experience and celebrate our relationship to the Creator.
>
> From this Franciscan, cosmic vision, we invite all to abandon their excessive consumer mentality: the accumulation of goods, the plunder and abuse of nature. In the same way, we urge them to have a simple lifestyle, to foster the spirit of fraternity in their relationships, to be in solidarity with and have respect for all life forms. We want to defend and protect all creatures, especially those that are endangered.

To put it in the terms of Elizabeth Johnson (*America*, 4/16/2001), our response to nature can take at least three forms: "*the contemplative response* [that] gazes on the world with eyes of love rather than with an arrogant, utilitarian stare ... the *ascetic response* [that] practices discipline in using the things of Earth ... [and] the *prophetic response* [that] moves us to action on behalf of justice for Earth."[8]

---

[7] Delio, et al, *Care for Creation*, 205.

[8] Adam Zagajewski, "A Quick Poem," *Mysticism for Beginners*, trans. Clare Cavanagh (New York: Farrar, Straus and Giroux, 1997), 7.

D. QUESTIONS

1. Do I view my relationship to creation as part of my journey to God?

2. What aspects of Francis' spirituality can help me become more ecologically sensitive?

3. What am I doing to nurture a more familial relationship with the environment?

4. Where have I taken for granted God's good gifts in this world? Who goes without these gifts?

5. How do I view environmentalists, developers, animal rights activists, vegetarians, factory farms, etc.?

E. FURTHER READINGS

Delio, Ilia, Keith Warner, Pamela Wood. *Care for Creation: a Franciscan spirituality of the Earth*. Cincinnati: St. Anthony Messenger Press, 2008.

Delio, Ilia. *A Franciscan View of Creation: Learning to Live in a Sacramental World*, St. Bonaventure: Franciscan Institute Publications, 2003.

Eric Doyle. *"The Song of the Brotherhood and Sisterhood."* St. Bonaventure: Franciscan Institute Publications, 1997.

Dawn M. Nothwehr. *Franciscan Theology of the Environment: An Introductory Reader*. Quincy: Franciscan Press, 2002.

Elise Saggau, ed. *Franciscans and Creation: What Is Our Responsibility?* St. Bonaventure: Franciscan Institute Publications, 2003.

F. Picture Credits

Sermon to the Birds, Scene XV, Upper Church, Assisi

Unit Fourteen

The Franciscan Role in the Church

CONTENTS

From the Franciscan Sources

A.   Introduction

B.   Survey

C.   Information

D.   Questions

E.   Bibliography

F.   Picture Credits

FROM THE FRANCISCAN SOURCES

> The brothers' [and sisters'] way of life among the people [Francis said,] "should be such that whoever hears or sees them glorifies and praises the heavenly Father with dedication."
>
> For his great desire was that he, as well as his brothers [and sisters], would abound in such great deeds for which the Lord would be praised. He used to tell them: "As you announce peace with your mouth, make sure that greater peace in in your hearts. Let no one be provoked to anger or scandal through you, but may everyone be drawn to peace, kindness, and harmony through your gentleness. For we have been called to this: to heal the wounded, bind up the broken, and recall the erring" (L3C 58).

A. INTRODUCTION

In the *Legend of the Three Companions*, we read about Francis's call to repair God's Church:

> While he was walking by the church of San Damiano, he was told in the Spirit to go inside for a prayer. Once he entered, he began to pray intently before an image of the Crucified Savior, which spoke to him in a tender and kind voice: "Francis, don't you see that my house is being destroyed? Go, then, and rebuild it for me" (L3C 13).

Commenting on Francis's manner of rebuilding, Thomas of Celano (1C 18) quotes St. Paul, "No one can lay a foundation other than the one that has been laid, namely, Jesus Christ" (1 Cor. 3:11). As collaborators with God we are invited to make real God's reign in our world. Francis's plan for rebuilding, his architectural drawings, if you will, are no more beautifully nor profoundly articulated that in his call for his family-in-Christ to heal the wounded, bind up the broken, and recall the erring. We must continue to reflect on this mission, if we want to fulfill the task of rebuilding the house of Christ. In doing so, we must humbly be the Church that Jesus has envisioned, in the spirit of Pope Paul VI's exhortation in *Evangelii nuntiandi*:

- By assisting the Church to become more Gospel-centered and oriented to the Reign of God.

- By helping people to find a protective home and kindly shelter in the church.[1]

B. SURVEY

This unit, composed of two parts, reflects on some aspects of the Church which are in constant need of conversion and evangelization. It then deals with Franciscan criteria for evangelization: the Gospel; love as the motive for action; commitment to the poor; and the willingness to share our faith with the unchurched. These concerns are addressed in an attempt to provide clues for incarnating the Franciscan mission today so as to announce peace through healing words, binding the broken, and recalling the erring.

C. INFORMATION

In the whole history of the Church, rarely has there been a call to mission so clear as this call heard by Francis of Assisi. The call is a demand for growth and change from within the Church itself but Francis and his companions did not hold positions of authority and power within the Church. So Francis, inspired by the Holy Spirit, devised a new approach: to renew the Church from within, and thus to impact every area of life. The early sources have fascinating reports about this movement for renewal, similar to that of the early Church reported in the

---

[1] Paul VI, *Evangelii nuntiandi* (Washington: Publications Office, United States Catholic Conference, 1976), #6.

The Franciscan Role in the Church

Acts of the Apostles. They show what happens when people allow themselves to be evangelized within the Church.

Like Francis, we answer a call from God, and we follow the impules of the Holy Spirit. It is not so far-fetched to expect Franciscan-minded people to begin new impulses and movements in the Church, and to carry the Church along into an ongoing process of conversion and evangelization. The Holy Spirit's action within us is central to this process, as the Vatican II document *Ad Gentes* so clearly attests:

> In various manners the Holy Spirit awakens the missionary spirit in the Church. It is not seldom that this same Spirit precedes the action of those who are charged to lead the life of the Church.[2]

The task of evangelization proves to be easier when those who posses authority and power within the Church exhibit a trust and confidence in the working of the Holy Spirit among all of the People of God. Obedience to ecclesial structures and programs must always be related to the impulses of the Spirit of God, who works not only in structures, but also in people. Blind subservience must not have a place in a Church governed by the Holy Spirit, especially among those who are called to the process of rebuilding God's house. On the other hand, the Franciscan-inspired person does not set his or her opinions, insights, or experiences against defined Church teachings. The Franciscan impulse is not to make statements, but to live a life that imitates Francis's call to be peacemakers among the people. Francis was a man of profound courtesy and respect: a virtue desperately needed by anyone who wishes to follow his way.

Francis was also a man of courage. This virtue led him to create new ways of preaching the faith that sprung from his conviction that what he offered comes as a gift from the Spirit of God: "The Most High himself revealed to me" (Test 14). The gift given became the gift that was passed on. Because of this,

---

[2] *Ad Gentes Divinitus*, Decree on the Church's Missionary Activity, *Vatican Council II. The Conciliar and Post Conciliar Documents*, ed. Austin Flannery, O.P. (Collegeville: Liturgical Press, 1979), 846, #29.

Francis respected the Church and others, inviting every brother and sister to be aware of his and her own personal charism. This respect, due to the Spirit's influence in every person, was imprinted on Francis's and Clare's Rules, both of which promote a sensitive insight into the workings of the Spirit when discerning, the missionary vocation of a brother (LR XII) or a vocation in general (ER II and XVI; FLCl III:1).

In *The Little Flowers of St. Francis* we find the story of the three robbers who were chased away by the guardian of the house. Hearing this, Francis put the guardian to a severe test, as we discover in the following lines:

> Since you acted against charity and against the example of Jesus Christ, I order you under holy obedience to take right now this sack of bread and jug of wine which I begged. Go and look carefully for those robbers over the mountains and valleys until you find them. And offer them all this bread and this wine for me. And then kneel down before them and humbly accuse yourself of your sin and cruelty. And then ask them in my name not to do those evil things anymore, but to fear God, and not to offend their neighbors. And if they do so, I promise them that I will supply them with provisions for their needs and I will give them food and drink all the time. (LFl 26)

The theme of this story became a Franciscan value encoded in the *Rule*: "Whoever comes to them, friends or foe, thief or robber, let them be received with kindness" (ER VII:14).

This principle has much to do with Francis's concept of poverty: whoever has no possessions has no need for defense against others. Over and above this poverty concept, however, is Francis's behavior. It shows the fundamental goodness of a heart that embraces all humanity – indeed, all creation – and discovers, even in wrong behavior, the human person who needs nothing more than loving kindness. One is reminded of the "Parable of the Lost Sheep" (Lk. 15:1-7). More than anyone else, the outcast is the person who needs special attention and love, not condemnation.

In *Evangelii nuntiandi*, Paul VI reminds us that the Church "has a constant need of being evangelized, if she wishes to retain freshness, vigor and strength in order to proclaim the Gospel."[3] This statement refers to everyone and everything in the Church: bishops and laity, structures and traditions. As people who desire to keep the Franciscan message alive, we must make ourselves the first recipients of the Pope's message: we must hear and receive the Gospel in order to share the Gospel.

The Franciscan mission within the Church does not consist in defending the faith against outside forces; there are other groups with that charism. The Franciscan challenge is to accept Francis's call to heal and to mend and to call according to the Gospel. As loyal and committed Catholics (LR I and II), we have the duty to challenge the Church to be imbued with these Gospel values, even to the point of prophetically speaking out when the Church is seen to act against such values. This demands the courtesy and courage of which we have already spoken.

We need, then, some Franciscan principles for this process of "evangelization from within." Among the criteria are:

- The Gospel

While loyal to the Church and respectful of her leaders, Francis concentrated his energy on sharing a new form of life according to the Gospel for everyone. He rejected all attempts to pin down the Good News under a mass of legal regulations, ordinances or prescriptions. He forbade his brothers to annotate, gloss or provide further comments on the *Rule*. Accordingly, the primary criterion for the life and work of the Franciscan brothers and sisters in the Church is embracing the Good News of Jesus Christ, making it relevant for the modern world. Concretely living the Gospel means to "be Church," to be among the people and to live in the world in the Spirit of Jesus.

- Love as the principle of action

---

[3] *Apostolic Exhortation of Paul VI: On Evangelization in the Modern World – Evangelii nuntiandi* (St. Paul Book and Media, n/d).

Pope John Paul II has repeatedly emphasized that the aim of all missionary activity is the proclamation of the Gospel to the whole world[4]. In the Vatican II decree "*Ad Gentes*," the Church defines herself as follows:

> According to its nature, the Church is missionary. It is sent forth as an envoy, because it derives its origin from the mission of the Son himself and from the mission of the Holy Spirit, according to the plan of the Father. This plan arises from the source of all love, the will of the Father.[5]

The Gospel is full of examples of Jesus' actions that reveal God's love for people. It also clearly shows that deeds are more important than words. Jesus taught the meaning of love by parables, such as the parable of the Good Samaritan, which shows in a very concrete way what it means to love one's neighbor. Thus, love is revealed as the foundation of any rebuilding project for the Franciscan. The Gospel is for living: it must be heard, believed, and lived to be life-giving. Have we learned how to live according to the Gospel? With the Good News as our guide, we need to examine ourselves on how we deal with the people we meet daily and on the quality of relationships we establish with them. We may discover that we fall short in comparison to the love that Jesus showed in word and deed thus pointing out an area where we need to be newly and courageously evangelized.

Every relationship must be rooted in the love of God. Jesus can be present only when the love which bound him to the Father is manifested in the lives of those who confess his name. When Jesus was about to confer the supreme mission on Peter, he solemnly asked him three times: "Simon, son of John, do you love me?" (Jn. 21:15-17). This questioning of Peter by Jesus clearly shows the kind and quality of relationship that should distiguish the pastors who have charge of the faithful; indeed, it should distinguish anyone who is engaged ina ministry in the Church. It is as if Jesus were saying to Peter – and to us:

---

[4] John Paul II. *Ecclesia in Asia*. 11/6/99, #42.
[5] *Ad Gentes*, #2.

"If you love me, then carry out my mission entrusted to you by ministering to my people."

Scripture is full of stories of people who discovered their true selves through their encounters with Jesus and their relationships with him. A good example is Zaccheus, the tax collector, who climbed a tree to see Jesus. Jesus did not pass by Zaccheus. He stopped, changed his plans and entered the house of Zaccheus. This encounter so moved Zaccheus that he pledged to distribute his wealth. Jesus then commented: "Today salvation is come to this house, because this is what it means to be a son of Abraham" (Luke 19:9). Nowhere in this account does Jesus refer directly to God. He simply informed Zaccheus that he wanted to stay in his house, and Zaccheus welcomed him. This simple gesture of hospitality had a far-reaching effect: Zaccheus's conversion.

From the events recounted in the New Testament, we can draw three conclusions. First, just as Jesus acted out of love for God and made the mandate of Peter dependent on his love for God, every Christian act must be rooted in the Good News of the life, death and resurrection of Jesus Christ. Jesus made Peter's mission dependent on his public admission of love to emphasize the fundamental precondition of all pastoral commitment. Peter and all his successors are expected to maintain a relationship of love with Christ and so lead others to God. Secondly, Jesus' message is clear one should assume pastoral activity only in the name of Jesus. Thirdly, we act in the name of Jesus when we understand the power that is released in us through God's love, putting this power into practice in relationships and actions.

- Life with the poor

To the question, "Who is the greatest in the Kingdom of Heaven," Jesus centered his response around children: in becoming like little children we recover the capacity to trust and to love. Jesus also warned that this capacity to love can be harmed and even destroyed because children are so powerless (cf. Matt 18:1-6).

Like the poor and marginalized discussed earlier, children receive special attention from Jesus and they are a priority for our evangelizing commitment: "Whoever receives such a child for my sake, receives me" (Matt 18:5). Likewise, Jesus uttered his severest condemnation against those who destroy children's innate ability to love and to trust. "It would be better for anyone who leads astray one of these little ones who believe in me, to be drowned with a millstone around his neck, in the depths of the sea" (Matt 18:6). Thus, our evangelizing efforts must be focused on the poor.

- Concern for the unchurched

Today we are faced with a new missionary situation. Large numbers of people are alienated from the Church. Many, while believing the Good News of Jesus, no longer feel at home in the institutional Church. Large sectors of the population in many countries live outside the Church. Our age has been described as "the post-Christian era." This may be particularly true of teens and young adults, many of whom have been described as "distant" or non-practicing Catholics. Consequently we are not only confronted with the task of "primary evangelization" also of re-evangelization. Thus, there is a need for people who are willing to cross beyond the conventional boundaries of Church, to open new paths of pastoral and apostolic service.

The same commision has been given to us Franciscan women and men as was given to St. Paul:

> I ... designate you as my servant and as a witness to what you have seen of me and what you will see of me. I have delivered you from this people and from the nations, to open the eyes of those to whom I am sending you, to turn them from darkness to light and from the dominion of Satan to God; that through their faith in me they may obtain the forgiveness of their sins and a portion among God's people (Acts 26:16b-18).

Similarly, Francis tells us: "I have done what is mine; may Christ teach you what is yours!" (2C 214).

D. QUESTIONS

1. How are Franciscans called to rebuild the Church today? What in your community/ministry needs renewal/re-formation?

2. To what end does Jesus call people to new life?

3. Where have you met "unchurched people" in society, in the Church, in your community?

4. Can Franciscan spirituality be a prophetic stance in the world/church today? In what areas would it exercise such a role?

5. Is the Gospel message of Francis still being proclaimed? How?

6. Can we be faithful to the Gospel and to our vocation as rebuilders of the Church for a new millenium if we do not become more and more visionaries and apostles of a global Church?

E. BIBLIOGRAPHY

Chinnici, Joseph P. *When Values Collide: The Catholic Church, Sexual Abuse, and the Challenges of Leadership*. Maryknoll: Orbis, 2010.

Fulton, John et al. *Young Catholics at the New Millennium: The Religion and Morality of Young Adults in Western Countries*, Dublin: University College Dublin Press, 2000.

Scherer, John & Bevens, Stephen. *New Directions in Mission and Evangelization*, three volumes: Basic Statements, Theological Foundations, and Faith & Culture, Maryknoll, NY: Orbis Press, 1992-1999.

F. PICTURE CREDITS

Santa Croce Sacristy Panels Quatrefoils: "Dream of Innocent III"

APPENDIX

Appendix

A. ABBREVIATIONS

Writings of Saint Francis

Adm	Admonitions
BlL	A Blessing for Brother Leo
CtC	The Canticle of the Creatures
CtExh	The Canticle of Exhortation
1 Frg	Fragments of Worchester Manuscript
2 Frg	Fragments of Thomas of Celano
3 Frg	Fragments of Hugh of Digne
Lt Ant	A Letter to Brother Anthony of Padua
1Lt Cl	First Letter to the Clergy (Earlier Edition)
2Lt Cl	Second Letter to the Clergy (Later Edition)
1LtCus	The First Letter to the Custodians
2LtCus	Second Letter to the Custodians
1 LtF	The First Letter to the Faithful
2 LtF	The Second Letter to the Faithful
LtL	A Letter to Brother Leo
LtMin	A Letter to a Minister
LtOrd	A Letter to the Entire Order
LtR	A Letter to the Rulers of the Peoples
ExhP	Exhortation to the Praise of God
PrOF	A Prayer Inspired by the Our Father
PrsG	The Praises of God
OfP	The Office of the Passion
PrCr	The Prayer before the Crucifix
ER	The Earlier Rule (*Regula non bullata*)
LR	The Later Rule (*Regula bullata*)
RH	The Rule for Hermitages
SalBV	A Salutation of the Blessed Virgin Mary
Test	The Testament
TPJ	True and Perfect Joy

Appendix

Fransicscan Sources

1C	The Life of Saint Francis by Thomas Celano
2C	The Rememberence of the Desire of a Soul
3C	Treatise on the Miracles by Thomas of Celano
LCh	The Legend for Use in the Choir
Off	The Divine Office of Saint Francis by Julian of Speyer
LJS	The Life of Saint Fracis by Julian of Speyer
VL	The Versified Life of Saint Francis by Henri d'Avranches
1-3JT	The Praises by Jacopone da Todi
DCom	The Divine Comedy by Dante Alighieri
TL	The Tree of Life by Ubertino da Casale
1MP	The Mirror of Perfection (Smaller Version)
2MP	The Mirror of Perfection (Larger Version)
HTrb	The Book of Chronicles or of the Seven Tribulations by Angelo of Clareno
ScEx	The Sacred Exchange between Saint Francis and Lady Poverty
AP	Anonymous of Perugia
L3C	The Legend of the Three Companions
LP	The Legend of Perugia
AC	The Assisi Compilation
UChL	An Umbrian Choir Legend
1-4Srm	The Sermons of Bonaventure
LMj	The Major Legend by Bonaventure
LMn	The Minor Legend by Bonaventure
BPr	The Book of Praises by Bernard of Besse
ABF	The Deeds of Saint Francis and His Companions
IntR	The Intention of the Rule
OL	An Old Legend
WSF	The Words of Saint Francis
WBC	The Words of Brother Conrad
LFl	The Little Flowers of Saint Francis (*Fioretti*)
KnSF	The Kinship of Saint Francis
ChrTE	The Chronicle of Thomas of Eccleston
ChrJG	The Chronicle of Jordan of Giano

The Writings of Saint Clare

1LAg	The First Letter to Agnes of Prague
2LAg	The Second Letter to Agnes of Prague
3LAg	The Third Letter to Agnes of Prague
4LAg	The Fourth Letter to Agnes of Prague
LEr	The Letter to Ermentrude of Bruges
RCl	The Rule
TestCl	The Testament
BCl	The Blessing

The Writings that Concern Saint Clare and the Poor Ladies

Form Viv	The Form of Life Given by Saint Francis
JdV	Witness of Jacques de Vitry
1PrPov	The Privilege of Poverty of Pope Innocent III
EpHon	The Letter of Pope Honorius III to Cardinal Hugolino
RHug	The Rule of Cardinal Hugolino
LHug	The Letter of Cardinal Hugolino
UltVol	The Last Will of Saint Francis Written for the Poor Ladies
LGreg	The Letter of Pope Gregory IX
LRay	The Letter of Cardinal Raynaldus
2PrPov	The Privilege of Poverty of Pope Gregory IX
LAgA	The Letter of Saint Agnes of Assisi
Mand	The Mandate
RInn	The Rule of Pope Innocent IV
Proc	Acts of the Process of Canonization of Saint Clare
Not	The Notification of the Death of Saint Clare
BC	The Bull of Canonization
LegCl	The Legend of Saint Clare